ARISE YE SONS AND DAUGHTERS

Robert A. Allen
and Randy L. Miller

Dedication

To all the "sons and daughters" God brought to Pillsbury Baptist Bible College through the years.

"To God be the glory, great things He has done."
(Crosby)

ARISE YE SONS AND DAUGHTERS

Robert A. Allen and Randy L. Miller

"The Lord hath done great things for us;
whereof we are glad."
Psalm 126:3

"O God, we stand in awe of the work which Thou
hast wrought."
Dr. Monroe Parker

While the following stories explore events which happened in the lives of many individuals—all the glory belongs to God.

For more than fifty years God used the influence of Pillsbury Baptist Bible College to mold the lives and futures of over five thousand students, staff and faculty. It is our desire to share these stories to the praise of His glory.

It is our hope that this volume will be followed by several expanded editions as those who studied and lived on the "hills of Owatonna" contribute their stories of what God has done in and through them. At the end of this book you will find a questionnaire which will aid in the completion of that goal. Please send it in so that your story can be included in future expansions. Updates are also welcomed.

PILLSBURY COLLEGE HYMN
Words by Dr. Monroe Parker
Music by Dr. Thelma Cedarholm

"In southern Minnesota, ten thousand lakes of blue,
On the hills of Owatonna, 'neath skies of azure hue,
There stands a mighty fortress of the truth our fathers taught.
O God, we stand in awe of the work with Thou hast
wrought."

"In ancient ivied halls 'mid culture's pleasing grace,
Within these hallowed walls our Lord shall have first place.
O teach us, Lord, Thine inspired Word written by men of
old,
Moved by Thy Holy Spirit, Dearer far than gold."

"Ten thousand men and demons attack our cause forsooth;
We're fully panoplied, girt 'round the loins with truth,
In breastplate of righteousness, made ready our feet are shod
With thorough preparation, the gospel of peace with God."

"Then with the mighty shield of faith we quench each fiery
dart;
O fill us, Holy Spirit, and ne'er from us depart.
In helmet of salvation we wield the Spirit's sword,
A weapon never failing, God's everlasting Word."

"Arise, ye sons and daughters, Pillsbury warriors all!
From jungles far away, from town and hamlet small
Come cries of souls sin-bound and doomed to endless woe.
All your hearts with love aflame, Arise and to them go!"

ARISE YE SONS AND DAUGHTERS

"The Lord hath done great things for us;
whereof we are glad."

Psalm 126:3

Jeff and Marilyn (Steffek) Alexander

Students: 1961-1965

Jeff Alexander accepted the call to pastor Galeton
Baptist Church after graduation. He married Marilyn
Steffek in June of 1967. They moved to Minnesota to
attend Central Baptist Theological Seminary and Jeff
became the pastor of Bellaire Baptist in White Bear
Lake. The name of the church became Victory Baptist,
and Alexanders stayed there until 1976. In that year he

became an assistant to former Pillsbury professor Ray Newton at Bible Baptist Church of Terre Haute, Indiana. Feeling the call of God to evangelism, Jeff traveled as Evangelist and chalk artist from 1979-1990. Relocating to Denver, he worked for Alexander Estate Homes when not on the road. At South Sheridan Baptist Church Jeff taught adult Sunday School and served as a deacon.

In 1990, the Alexanders moved to Lamar, Colorado, to pastor the Calvary Baptist Church where they have remained to the present time. God has given them six children. Jeff also drives bus for Lamar school district activities. He has also served as a board member of the Colorado Association of Christian Schools.

Jeff has developed and managed websites for several businesses and organizations including Calvary Baptist (www.cause-of God.com). He wrote a book about his journey to understand the doctrines of grace called *Predestined for Heaven? Yes!* "I am blessed to know that Jesus Christ is a great Savior of sinners," writes Jeff, "and that He saved me and desires that I know Him by enabling me through His Spirit and Word to love Him and serve Him. He is ever faithful and true!"

Arthur W. Allen

Board of Trustees: 1966 – 1983 (Ex-officio)

Faculty: 1970-1973

Before moving to Minnesota, Arthur W. Allen served as a Church Planting Missionary for the Intermountain Baptist Fellowship. He aided in the starting of more than thirty churches in Montana, Wyoming and South Dakota as well as serving pastorates in Baker, Dillon and Laurel, Montana, and Newcastle, Wyoming.

Arthur Allen served as an ex-officio member of the Board of Trustees by virtue of his position as Executive Secretary of the Minnesota Baptist Association. He also taught part-time at the college for a number of years. The 1969 *Northern Light* was dedicated to him with the ascription "Valiant for the Truth." It said in part, "He has the zeal of an evangelist and the burning missionary vision of a spiritual pioneer."

After leaving Minnesota, Arthur Allen joined the faculty of Mountain States Bible College in Great Falls, Montana, teaching Pastorology, Homiletics and Church Planting. From there, he and his wife Verna moved to Laurel, Montana. First Baptist Church in Laurel had been planted when Arthur served as Field Director for the Inter-Mountain Baptist Fellowship. He had served as their pastor from 1955 to 1966 and was welcomed back as an assistant pastor by Pillsbury Alumnus David Smith. He died in Laurel in 1995.

Dr. Allen was known for his church planting, his Bible Land Tours and his love for rocks. Numerous churches in Montana, Wyoming and Minnesota were started through his leadership. He was one of the founders of Castle Rock Baptist Camp. He led twenty-nine tours to Bible Lands. There was always a rock tumbler running in his garage, alongside a diamond blade saw and equipment for polishing semi-precious gem stones. He would give agate rings, necklaces and bolo ties as gifts, along with a reminder of the Creator God who had hidden this beauty in the rocks of the earth.

The hobby opened many doors, generating invitations to speak in science classes and exchanging of gemstones with people in Egypt, Israel, Greece, Thailand and other countries he visited. His travels and experiences were shared with his family in an auto-biographical memoir called *Still Climbing*.

Carmen (Odens) Allen

Student: 1967-1971

Faculty: 1988-1996

During the years immediately after graduation Carmen remained busy raising three preacher's kids in Lake Benton, Minnesota. Tammy would join Chad, Wendy and Kent later in Colorado. When the Allens moved to Ordway, Colorado, Carmen trained a traveling choir at Ordway Baptist Christian School and taught musicians who gained national honors in Accelerated Christian Education competition. She taught private piano while Bob served on the faculty at Liberty University in Lynchburg, Virginia, and then became a combined fourth-through-sixth grade class teacher at Bible Baptist Christian School in Missoula, Montana.

The Allens returned to Owatonna in 1987. Carmen joined the music faculty, directed the handbell choir and the Hallelujah Voices and completed her Master of Music degree in composition at Minnesota State University in Mankato. While working on the degree a surprise came to the Allen household with the addition of their youngest son, Christopher. 1996 brought a move to Baptist Bible College in Clarks Summit, Pennsylvania where Carmen joined the music faculty as an adjunct. From 2002 to 2016, during her husband's years as pastor in Maxwell, Nebraska, she taught music theory at Mid-Plains Community College and also conducted the Sandhills Symphony Orchestra.

Carmen operates a home-based composition and arranging business called ARIA music. She is active in the music ministry at Fourth Baptist Church of Minneapolis.

David and Cindy (Odens) Allen

Student: David – 1969-1973

Student: Cindy – 1971-1975

After David Allen and Cindy Odens were married in 1975, they lived in Minneapolis, attending Fourth Baptist Church and then Valley Baptist Church. In 1978 they moved to Colorado Springs, Colorado. Dave started a painting and wallpaper hanging business and Cindy taught first and second grade at Cornerstone Christian Academy. They both served in various ministries at Cornerstone Baptist Church.

In 1982 the Allens moved to Laurel, Montana. Dave became the Administrator at Yellowstone Valley Christian School, under the auspices of First Baptist Church. They have been active in the music, sound, and other ministries of the church since that time.

Dave began working in the insurance industry in 1989, focusing on life insurance and individual/group health insurance. Their son Eric has since joined with him to form Allen and Associates Insurance.

Cindy has taught private piano, various grades at Yellowstone Valley Christian School and served as the Council Secretary for the City of Laurel for twenty years. They have four children, four "in-loves," and fourteen grandchildren. Ethan and Michelle Allen serve with CRU on college campuses in North Carolina. Eric and Candi Allen live in Billings, Montana where Eric works with David at Allen and Associates. Emily and Chris Haynes live in Washington and serve at Galilee Baptist Church and Cascade Vista Baptist School. Kirk and Elise Williams live in Billings and are entrepreneurs at Zato Marketing, eMarie Photography, and BHive Workspace. All four of their children graduated from Pillsbury as well as spouses Chris and Kirk.

"We are thankful to live in Big Sky Country," write the Allens, "and thankful that our children and spouses love the Lord and serve Him in their lives and their churches."

Dorinda "DJ" (Lind) Allen

Student: 1995-2000

Dorinda Lind married Kent Allen in June of 1997. They lived in Minneapolis until 2006. DJ taught math at Fourth Baptist Christian School and coached volleyball for three years in Brooklyn Center. Their first daughter, Lyric was born in 2000, followed by Lanie in 2001. Lance followed in 2004.

2006 found the Allens in North Platte, Nebraska, when Kent went to work for Union Pacific Railroad. Dorinda taught high school math in Maxwell, and they welcomed their fourth child, Landon, in 2009. Beginning in 2011 her teaching position moved to Hershey High School and she was also able to pursue her master's degree during that time.

In the summer of 2017 they moved to Lincoln, Nebraska, so DJ could teach Math at Lincoln Christian School. She completed her Masters in Instruction Technology from the University of Kearney in May of 2018.

Through the years the Allens have served in youth ministry in the churches where they have attended. "My education training at Pillsbury helped me form the conviction that we serve a God of order," says DJ. "I believe He created everyone with the ability to learn math, and it is my passion to discover how each student learns, helping them reach their fullest potential."

Dorothy Allen (See Dorothy Freerksen)

Emily Allen (See Chris and Emily Haynes)

Ethan Allen

Student: 1995-1999

Ethan came to Pillsbury from Laurel, Montana. After graduation he enrolled in the United States Sports Academy in Daphne, Alabama, and earned his masters degree. From there he moved to North Carolina and became part of the Charlotte Eagles soccer organization under Missionary Athletes International. From 2009 to

2012 he served as an assistant soccer coach at Liberty University in Lynchburg, Virginia.

In 2011 Ethan married Michelle Edwards and God has given them two children. Since 2012 they have served on several college campuses as staff with Campus Crusade for Christ.

Kent Allen

Student: 1993-1997

Kent married Dorinda "DJ" Lind in 1997. They lived in the Minneapolis area for a time and then moved to North Platte, Nebraska, where Kent took a position with Union Pacific Railroad. From there he transitioned to several other areas of business in Internet Technology and Retail Business. He served as a youth pastor for three years. When DJ accepted a Math teaching position at Lincoln Christian High School they moved to Lincoln, Nebraska, where Kent again found a position in retail, selling technology. The Allens have four children, Lyric, Lanie, Lance and Landon. Their oldest started college in the fall of 2018.

Kent has had many opportunities to mentor young people. In addition to being a youth pastor, he has worked extensively with a mentorship program in the public schools. He has also experienced the blessing of being able to share spiritual insight with the friends of his children as they work through situations in their own lives. He and Dorinda often rejoice in the fact that God has given their family good health, a blessing often overlooked until issues arise.

Peggy Allen (See Peggy Cadwell)

Robert A. Allen

Student: 1965-1969

Faculty: 1969-1972; 1987-1996

After completing his MDiv at Central Baptist Theological Seminary and his MA at Minnesota State University of Mankato, Bob accepted the pastorate of the First Baptist Church of Lake Benton, Minnesota. In 1976 God called them to Colorado where he became principal of Ordway Baptist Christian School. From there they moved to Lynchburg, Virginia. At Liberty University he filled the position of Drama Coordinator and traveled with the King's Players drama team.

Western roots called the Allens back to Montana and a ministry at Bible Baptist Church in Missoula, Montana. During those years his first book, *Billy Sunday: Home Run to Heaven* was published. Returning to Pillsbury in 1987, Bob became chair of the Communications

Department, organized the Pillsbury Players and directed campus dramatic productions.

In 1996 Baptist Bible College of Pennsylvania invited Bob to become chair of their Pastorology Division. The availability of Baptist Bible Seminary made it possible for him to complete a Doctor of Ministry degree and also serve on the pastoral staff at Grace Bible Church of Dunmore.

Bob continued to write during his years in Pennsylvania and then Nebraska. He has published sixteen books and numerous articles, plays, and short stories as well as writing curriculum for Union Gospel Press for over forty years. From 2002 to 2016 he pastored a growing rural church in Maxwell, Nebraska, and saw the debt-free completion of an addition to the building more than doubling their ministry capacity. The Allens now live in New Hope, Minnesota, where Bob works at free-lance writing. He recently completed a five-part devotional book series called *Dare to Walk on Water*. He teaches at Twin Cities Bible Institute and in the Adult ministry at Fourth Baptist Church. In the spring of 2019 Bob was hired as an adjunct at the University of Northwestern, St. Paul. He teaches Public Speaking in a department headed up by Pillsbury alumnus Dr. Jackie Glenny.

Tammy Allen (See Tammy Cress)

Wendy Allen (See Joe and Wendy Daniels)

Tom Andersen

Student: 1989-1992

Tom Andersen enrolled at Central Seminary after graduation to study Greek and Hebrew. He spent five years as a part-time on-air operator at WCTS and worked as a FedEx courier. Transferring to Texas, he completed an MABS at Dallas Theological Seminary.

For eleven years Tom served as Director of Operations at Need Him Ministries, an evangelistic response center. He managed multiple call centers and personally trained, equipped and managed hundreds of volunteers. Tom attended a small Baptist church east of Dallas for sixteen years, serving as pianist, youth worker and adult Sunday School teacher. At the present time he writes software for RightNow Media, a Christian video producer and church curriculum distributer. He also assists with the youth ministry at a large Baptist church in McKinney, Texas.

Jackie Anderson (See Jackie Glenny)

Glenn and Anita Andes

Student: Glenn 1975-1978

Student: Anita 1975-1979

Over the past thirty-nine years the Lord has blessed Glenn and Anita with seven children and four grandchildren. They have had the privilege of serving in pastoral ministry at three churches.

"We are not sufficient of ourselves to think of anything as being from ourselves, but our sufficiency is from God." (II Corinthians 3:5)

Bruce and Marsha (Reed) Andrejzchick

Student: 1975-1978

Staff: Bruce – 1977-1982

Staff: Marsha – 1980-1981

Bruce Andrejzchick worked on the Pillsbury radio station in 1975 with Larry Soblotne and later with Randy Miller when he became station manager. During the first few years they were a carrier current AM station which used the electrical wiring on campus as the antenna. Listeners could pick up the station in Old Main, both dorms and the parking lot. He loved to play the Sixteen Singing Men and male acapella groups.

Bruce married Pillsbury's school nurse, Marsha Reed, and accepted a job with the Bible Broadcasting Network in Gaffney, South Carolina. He had undergone a kidney transplant earlier in life, and health issues began to surface once again. He had to take anti-rejection medicine to keep his body from rejecting the transplant, but the medicine caused cancer cells to

Shelley Beth (Clapp) Ashley

Student: 1976-1980

Shelley Beth Clapp married Johnny Ashley, and they have one daughter named Amanda. They run a sheet metal business and serve the Lord at First Baptist Church in Elk City, Oklahoma.

Shelley has been blessed to facilitate a Divorce Recovery Group for the past twenty years. They have seen men and women come to Jesus Christ through that ministry as well as many who have rededicated their lives to the Lord. "God has turned difficulties and heartache into His name being glorified," writes Shelley. "No matter what life brings us, God gives grace and mercy to those who put their faith and trust in Him. Praise be to God for His marvelous work."

Rebecca "Becky" (Wichman) Atwood

Student: 1992-1996

From Owatonna, Becky moved home for a time and then settled in Mankato, Minnesota where she worked as a florist for three years. She met David Atwood at Hope Baptist Church and they were married in 2000. They moved to Rochester, Minnesota, and have attended Berean Community Church for nineteen years where they presently serve and do life together alongside other former Pillsbury friends. God has given them two children, Samuel and Gracelyn.

Becky served on the Camp Team at Pillsbury, which led her to work for three summers at High Point Camp in Geigertown, Pennsylvania. She feels that her "camping" experiences were instrumental in preparing her to serve in the middle school ministry at their church for over twelve years. God has also allowed her to serve musically by playing her saxophone and singing on their contemporary worship team. It has been a great blessing to have the entire family involved in music on some Sundays.

Becky currently works at the church as an office assistant, helping with organization, communications and publications. A highlight has been the experience of traveling to Haiti on several occasions, getting to know and grow relationships with the family of Christ on that island. "I am thankful for the strong Christian friends He placed in my life, many with whom I still stay in contact," Becky writes of her college days. "He has continued to place wonderful people around me who sharpen and challenge me in my faith journey."

Carol (Soutter) Baker

Student: 1969-1971, Graduated with the AA in 1971

Carol married Dick Baker after graduation in 1971. She continued on with her education and earned her MA in Library Science. The Bakers started two churches, one in Mohawk, New York, and another in Lafayette, Indiana. They have two children, Dawn and Carrie.

In 1978 the family moved to Oak Forest, Illinois, where Dick became assistant pastor. They served there for many years before moving to Northside Baptist Church in St. Petersburg, Florida. In both churches they filled numerous roles, often in the areas of music, choir and band.

For twenty-four years Carol served as the librarian at Northside Christian School in St. Petersburg, Florida. She has been published in the library sector and has also served as a State Convention speaker on various occasions. She retired from the library in 2017 and enjoys being the grandmother of three grandchildren.

Charles Baker

Student: 1961-1965

Academic Dean: 1984-1991

Charles Baker married Janice Hart in Laurel, Montana, in 1965. From Pillsbury, the Bakers moved to San Francisco, California. At San Francisco Baptist Seminary he earned his BD and ThM degrees. After graduation from seminary the Bakers planted a church in Sonora, California, and served as pastor from 1970-1976. Returning to San Francisco Baptist Seminary, Charles became a professor and Academic Dean, a position which he also filled at Pillsbury from 1984-1991. Moving from Owatonna back to California, he accepted the position of pastor at Highland Baptist Church in Hayward and then First Baptist Church of Pinole before retiring in 2012.

In addition to his work as senior pastor, Charles has been blessed to serve as interim pastor in seven churches. Maranatha Baptist Bible College honored him with a Doctor of Divinity degree. A highlight of ministry has been the opportunity to be involved in mission trips to Singapore, India, Russia, Ukraine and the Philippines.

Dick Baker

Student: 1968-1971

"We are blessed every day and thank the Lord for the education we got at Pillsbury," says Dick Baker. "The Bible aspect of that education is appreciated every week when I step into a pulpit or classroom to teach."

Dick married Carol Soutter right after graduation in 1971. He was ordained one year later and went on to earn his ThD. Their early ministry included two church-planting opportunities, one in Mohawk, New York, and one in Lafayette, Indiana. During those years their two daughters, Dawn and Carrie were born.

Their home church, Oak Forest Baptist Temple of Oak Forest, Illinois, invited Dick to return in 1978 as assistant pastor. For the next several years he did "about anything and everything," filling and enjoying the role of second man. In 1981 he had the honor of returning to the Pillsbury campus with their high school concert band of sixty-five musicians. They played a full concert in chapel and spent the night in the dorms with some great college students. From Illinois they moved to Northside Baptist Church in St. Petersburg, Florida.

Dick recently retired but continues to serve as an adult Bible class teacher at Northside Baptist Church in St. Petersburg, Florida. There they also participate in choir, duet and solo work as church musicians, something which has always played a major role in their lives. Dick has been a conference speaker, seminar speaker, band and choir director and has written a book. One of their greatest blessings has been enjoying their three grandchildren.

Janice "Jan" (Hart) Baker

Student: 1962-1965

Staff: 1984-1990

Janice Hart married Charles Baker on June 25, 1965, at First Baptist Church in Laurel, Montana. They moved to Oakland, California, where Chuck enrolled at San Francisco Baptist Seminary, graduating in 1970. They started Grace Baptist Church of Sonora, California and then returned to teach at San Francisco Seminary in 1976. While Charles served as the Academic Dean at Pillsbury, Janice worked in the Finance office. Back in California they ministered at Highland Baptist Church in Hayward and then First Baptist Church of Pinole before retirement in 2012. They moved to Pennsylvania for their retirement years.

Jan worked in children's ministry as well as serving as a Ladies Bible teacher. Other opportunities to serve came through AWANA, Vacation Bible School, and Joy Club. She has been a nanny, daycare assistant, church secretary, Christian school secretary and a kindergarten teacher. Throughout all their ministry it has been her desire to be a supportive wife to her husband's various ministries.

Eugene Ball

Staff Printer: 1989-1991

Eugene Ball served in the United States Air Force until his honorable discharge in 1957. He and his wife Dorothy were working with the youth at Normandale Baptist Church in Minneapolis when he was invited to become the printer at Pillsbury. He later served in the same position at Faith Baptist Bible College in Ankeny, Iowa.

Gene was an active and faithful member of Maranatha Baptist Church in Grimes, Iowa, when he died in 2014. His greatest passion was his faith in God and service to his Lord.

Bob Bardwell

Student: 1965-1969

After completing a successful career as a collegiate wrestler at Pillsbury, and preparing for ministry with a seminary degree, Bob Bardwell faced the greatest challenge of his young life. In 1973 a co-worker accidently dropped a Caterpillar earth-moving machine bucket on him. Seven hours of surgery took place at St. Mary's Hospital in Rochester, Minnesota. Six days of intensive care followed and then came the diagnosis. Two steel rods had been placed along his spine. He would be hospitalized for up to five months and would live the rest of his life as a paraplegic.

Bob had always been an athlete and he wasn't about to let that diagnosis change his plans. Since he no longer had the use of his legs, he worked to strengthen his arms and became a wheelchair racer. He has been involved in over one hundred marathons, each 26.2 miles in length. The National Wrestling Hall of Fame inducted him into its membership. He has written an inspirational autobiography called *The Marathons of Life*, and he shares his story as a motivational speaker across the country with a message entitled, "It's not what happens to you, it's what you do about it."

Three years after the accident, his father purchased forty acres of land west of Stewartville, Minnesota, and Ironwood Springs Christian Ranch was born. The camp now serves over 24,000 people annually, but Bob is particularly thrilled with its ministry to those with disabilities. In 1986 they started the National Wheelchair Sports Camp which has served well over one thousand physically challenged kids and adults. Five years ago, he worked with Colonel Chaplain John Morris to provide free weekend retreats for soldiers and their families. The project became known as "Operation Welcome Home," and more than a thousand families have participated. Bob has written a history of Ironwood Springs Christian Ranch called *Spreading Joy and Changing Lives*.

"When disaster strikes, and our plans seem to be laid to ruin," says Bob, "we have the choice to become a victim or a victor." Through the strength which only Christ can give (II Corinthians 12:10) he is living a life of creative triumph, rejoicing in the privilege of serving God, even from a wheelchair. Married to Jode in 1991, the Bardwells have four daughters, Hannah, and the triplets, Lydia, Birdie and Abigail. The girls all attend the University of Northwestern in St. Paul, Minnesota.

Crystal Barringer (See Crystal Grotzke)

Shane and Paula (Schmidtgal) Belding

Student: 1984-1989

Shane Belding met Pillsbury alumnus Paul Fosmark at the Fundamental Baptist Church of Saint John, New Brunswick, and was encouraged by Paul to attend Pillsbury when Shane didn't even know what a Bible College was. After a rocky start he met his future wife, Paula Schmidtgal, and "due to her excellent academic prowess my grades went up and my success at Pillsbury took a radical turn for the better," says Shane.

After graduation, Shane went on to complete two more degrees, an MDiv and a DMin. He and Paula entered pastoral ministry in 1994. The Lord has used him to restore two church ministries and also plant two churches which are fulfilling the great commission. They presently serve Victory Baptist Church in Fort Francis, Ontario, as pastor and wife. Shane has had the privilege of traveling throughout the world training pastors on behalf of several mission agencies.

Dr. Belding serves as Camp Director of Camp Haven, a rustic camp in northern Ontario. With the assistance of other pastors, he started the Pastoral Training Institute, a three-year modular training program which fills the gap for those who otherwise could not get their training at traditional Bible colleges due to cost and other obligations.

"I am thankful for how God used Pillsbury alumni to set the course for me to train for ministry and the faithful staff who were used to prepare me so I could go on for more training," writes Shane.

Darrell and Deb Bevis

Faculty: 1981-1991; 1997-2008

Darrell Bevis completed both his BA and his MA in Music at Bob Jones University in Greenville, South Carolina. He is one of several faculty members who served at Pillsbury on two separate occasions. The Bevis family moved to Owatonna in 1981 where Darrell began teaching in the Division of Music. He served as chairman of that Division, directed choir and prepared many of the summer traveling groups for their ministry. From 1991 to 1997 he served on the faculty at Faith Baptist Bible College in Ankeny, Iowa before returning to teach at Pillsbury in 1997. Darrell was on faculty when the college closed in 2008.

After Pillsbury, Darrell became Assistant Pastor at Grace Baptist Church of Panama City, Florida. His ministry responsibilities include worship, Christian Education and preaching. The church ordained him in 2016, and it has been his privilege since that time to preach about once a month.

Julia (Tindall) Bloom

Student: 1993-1995

Julia Tindall attended The Master's College for one semester in 1995 and then transferred to Bethel

University in St. Paul, Minnesota, where she graduated in 1997 with a bachelor's degree in music. She married Nathan Bloom and they lived in Minneapolis from 1998-2006 where she worked for Christians for Biblical Equality. Moving from there back to Owatonna, Julia served as artist-in-residence for Mars Hill Church.

Julia and Nathan began writing and recording songs soon after they were married. They produced their first album, called *Cabin of Love* which has been followed by many others. She has forty-four songs on her own channel on You Tube as well as another thirty on the Cabin of Love channel. All of her songs are licensed with a Creative Commons license so that other people are free to use them, perform them, or even re-invent them as they see fit.

During a short time in Colorado, Julia worked as music director at Mustard Seed Churches in Fort Collins. They moved back to St. Paul, Minnesota, in 2017. In addition to her song-writing and performing, Julia parents two children, and along with her husband has renovated several houses.

In 2016, Julia co-wrote (along with her father Larry Tindall and friend Matt Bissonette) a book called *Frankenchurch*. The book uses Mary Shelley's novel *Frankenstein* as a metaphor/lens through which to consider the life and history of the Christian church. She has also written for various in-house publications and traveled to represent Christians for Biblical Equality.

Teresa Bohren (See Teresa Griffin)

Brian Boldt

Student: 1974-1978

Brian followed a career in law enforcement after Pillsbury. He served as a city policeman in Plainview, Minnesota, and then as Minnesota State Trooper stationed in Owatonna. He coached baseball for Pillsbury and assisted with the girls' basketball team.

After thirty-one years in law enforcement, Brian retired. He drives school bus for a local company and coaches the varsity girls' basketball team at Owatonna Christian School. He has taken several missions trips over the years and is an active member of Grace Baptist Church. Both of their sons attended Pillsbury and still live nearby, Ben and Jill Boldt in Rochester and Bernie and Nicole Boldt in Oakland. They adopted a son named Brent who passed away in 2016.

The Boldts spent nearly forty years involved in the ministry of Pillsbury and miss both it and all the people who were a part of the college family. Brian loved the opportunity to share in the lives of many Comet athletes.

Deb (Frey) Boldt

Student: 1973-1977

Staff: 1985-2008

Faculty: 2001-2004

Deb Frey married Brian Boldt and stayed at home with their two sons, Ben and Bernie, until the need to pay tuition for Christian school sent her looking for a job. She began working at Pillsbury the same day Ben started kindergarten and worked at the college until it closed in 2008. To Deb, her position at Pillsbury was much more than a job. Students knew her door was always open, and their home was a place to hang out. "If they needed a hug, a shoulder to cry on, or someone to rejoice with, I was there for them," she recalls. The Boldts attended plays, concerts and athletic events, totally immersed in the Pillsbury scene.

The Boldts adopted Brent and raised him along with their sons. He passed away in 2016. Ben and Bernie both attended Pillsbury, and Bernie was one of the 2008 graduates, the final on-campus graduation before the school closed. So, Deb's father was in the first class at the college and her son was in the last.

Since Pillsbury, Deb considers her position as Grandma as her most important one. She also teaches at Owatonna Christian School and is active in Grace Baptist Church.

"When Dr. Huffman led in the last weeks of Pillsbury's existence," writes Deb, "he told us we'd all meet again in heaven on Pilly Corner. I think we will be too busy worshipping God to think about that then, but it's a sweet thing to think about while we are still here on earth, remembering with fondness the great days we shared at Pillsbury Baptist Bible College."

Edward Boll

Student: 1978-1983

Edward Boll served in the extension ministry of Grace Baptist Church in Owatonna during his college days. He participated in Saturday morning visitation for the church and was active in Prayer Band at the college. After graduation he attended Central Baptist Seminary.

Edward has counseled at summer camp and taught Vacation Bible School. He has spoken in several churches in South Dakota, North Dakota, Minnesota and Wisconsin. He has been a leader in the AWANA program in his home church and for twenty years has taught a Bible study at the Nursing Home and Assisted Living facility in Flandreau, South Dakota. "I plan to do a full Bible Commentary with several volumes," he writes. "I have started but just need to discipline more of my time."

Tom Bonner

Student: 1986-1992

Tom and his wife Loretta were married in Kalamazoo, Michigan, in 1978. They moved to Owatonna with their four children, Sarah, John, Jon and Mandy to attend Pillsbury. Tom finished his BA in elementary education with a minor in special education in 1992.

Tom loved teaching. He taught at a school in West Virginia, and then one in Chicago. In Georgia he spent twelve years teaching as well while dealing with renal failure. Along with his school teaching, he was active in children's ministries in the churches they attended and loved Vacation Bible School. He had the privilege of leading many children to the Lord.

Because of his illness, Tom was on home dialysis for three years. He passed away in 2016.

Doug and Diane (Nord) Bookman

Student: Doug -1964-1968

Student: Diane – 1969-1970

Faculty: 1973-1984

Doug came to Pillsbury from Rockford, Illinois, and completed his BA. The MDiv and ThM degrees were earned from Central Baptist Seminary, and the ThD from Dallas Theological Seminary. Immediately after Central, Doug served as pastor in Rock Falls, Wisconsin, before returning to Pillsbury in 1973. There he became head of the Bible Department and led study tours to Israel. He is remembered for his rabbit trails, and for being more interested in teaching students than in just covering material. Doug wrote many of the Pillsbury position papers which were published during those years.

Following his time at Pillsbury, Dr. Bookman taught and preached in local churches before joining the faculty of The Master's College in 1987. While there he conceived, designed, and implemented the IBEX program, a semester-abroad study program in Israel. In 1998 he joined the Friends of Israel as a national representative. Much of his ministry for the next decade focused on Israel and the Life of Christ. He led study trips to Israel and spoke at Bible Conferences across the United State and overseas.

In 2009, Doug joined the Shepherd's Theological Seminary faculty in Cary, North Carolina. He heads up student recruitment and teaches New Testament Exposition. Dr. Bookman enjoys leading numerous study trips to Israel, including an annual trip designed specifically for seminary students.

Doug and Diane have three children "aggressive in their faith" and ten grandchildren, all of whom are close-by. Doug describes Diane as "the world's best wife" and says, "our lines have fallen out in pleasant places." He continues to enjoy an active ministry with study tours to Israel, appreciates the opportunity to be reunited with a number of other Pillsbury alums at Shepherd, and writes that he is "healthy and strong in his dotage."

Karolyn Grace (Jorgensen) Boston

Student: 2008

Karolyn arrived on campus in the fall of 2008 as part of the last group of Pillsbury freshmen. She loved being there and ached when she found out it would all end. She finally decided to transfer to Northland

International University. "Dr. and Mrs. Huffman's visits were one of the highlights of each year," Karolyn writes. "Their love and care for us was huge and made me remember that this was all part of God's plan. I couldn't believe that they remembered each of us and took the time to be there for us."

Karolyn met Caleb Boston at Northland and they were married in 2013. Caleb completed a Master in Biblical Studies degree in preparation for the pastorate. That meant that they were at Northland the year it closed as well. In the fall of 2016 Caleb accepted the pastorate of Sand Creek Baptist Church of Jordan, Minnesota, a bi-vocational ministry. Their daughter, Britain Arielle was born in 2017.

"My goal is to live a life that oozes out the kind of love that Dr. and Mrs. Huffman showed," writes Karolyn. "The kind that appreciates each individual and hears them even when some are so vastly different from who I am. I am so thankful for my Pillsbury memories and for the wonderful fellow students, staff, and faculty who cared enough to invest and believe in me."

Bruce Brandenburg

Student: 1969-1973

After graduating from Pillsbury Bruce attended Central Seminary and received his MDiv degree in 1977. During those years he was assistant pastor at First Calvary Baptist of South St. Paul. He and Marnee were appointed as missionaries to Austria by Baptist Mid-Missions in 1977. They ministered in church-planting ministries in Vienna, Austria, from 1980-1982. Next, they planted Maranatha Freie Baptisten Gemeinde (Church) in Bad Heilbrunn, Germany, where they stayed until 1993.

Returning to Minneapolis, Bruce worked at the University of Minnesota-Minneapolis from 1994-1999 with Campus Bible Fellowship. In 2000 they moved back to Germany to plant an international church in Berlin.

2004 found the Brandenburgs back in the States, this time to care for aging parents. Bruce took a job as a carpenter/contractor. In the spring of 2013, he joined the ministry of Training Leaders International. The emphasis of TLI is on the theological training of national pastors world-wide. He has continued to work with them since that time.

Marnee "Mary" (Hanschen) Brandenburg

Student: 1968-1972

Marnee graduated from Pillsbury and then attended Rochester Junior College (now Winona State University) and completed her RN degree. While raising their family she has served as both a homemaker and an RN. The Brandenburgs were appointed by Baptist Mid-Missions to serve in Austria and after two years of deputation arrived on the field in 1980. They worked in church planting ministries until 1994 when they returned to Minneapolis to serve with Campus Bible Fellowship.

After another four years in Germany, the Brandenburgs returned to care for aging parents. Marnee became a research RN at the University of Minnesota. She stayed there until 2016 when she retired to assume an active role with Training Leaders International. Her ministry involves the discipling of missionary wives.

God has blessed the Brandenburgs with four children. John and his wife Stacie live in Charlotte, North Carolina. John is a senior graphic designer with the Billy Graham Evangelistic Association. Paul and Jodi live in Omaha, Nebraska where he is a special agent with the United States Secret Service. Sara and her husband, Steve Muhr, live in Maple Grove, Minnesota, and
Sara is an ICU RN at the University of Minnesota Hospital. Benjamin and his wife Tori live in Black Mountain, North Carolina. Ben is a history professor at Montreat College in Montreat, North Carolina.

Harriet Bratrud

Board of Trustees: 1958-1970

Trustee Emeritus

Dr. Harriet Bratrud was the wife of a prominent Minneapolis physician, Dr. Arthur F. Bratrud. They were long-time members of First Baptist Church of Minneapolis, pastored by Dr. W. B. Riley. After Dr.

Riley's death they moved their membership to Fourth Baptist and became staunch allies of Dr. R.V. Clearwaters. The Bratrud's home on Lake Calhoun was frequently used by the young people of Fourth for Sunday night singspirations.

By 1953, Mrs. Bratrud was a member of the board of the Conservative Baptist Fellowship and in 1955 she was added to the board of the Conservative Baptist Foreign Missionary Society. In 1961 she chaired the CBF Nominating Committee. Through the years she served on the boards of the Minnesota Baptist Convention, Central Baptist Theological Seminary and Pillsbury Baptist Bible College. She was also honored by being named a lifetime member of the Fundamental Baptist Fellowship Board.

Dr. Bratrud was a great financial contributor to the college, including scholarships given in her memory. One of the literary societies on campus was named after her and the 1962 *Northern Light* yearbook was dedicated to her. Because of her separatist convictions she was invited to be on the board of Baptist World Mission, headed by Dr. Monroe Parker. In 1966, Pillsbury awarded Mrs. Bratrud the honorary degree of Doctor of Humanities. The degree was conferred by President Dr. B. Myron Cedarholm who described her as "a well-known Bible teacher and speaker among women who had a far-reaching ministry among fundamental, separatist Baptists down through the years."

Dr. Arthur Bratrud died just one year after his retirement. Dr. Harriet Bratrud suffered a stroke in 1967. She died in 1986 at Maranatha Home, operated by the Minnesota Baptist Convention. She was 93.

Ron and Kathie (Hoehm) Brewer

Students: 1966-1970

Ron and his wife Kathie lived in Sleepy Eye, Minnesota, where Ron pastored the Calvary Baptist Church from 1978-1985. He became a missionary with Baptist International Evangelistic Ministries, serving in Eastern Europe. With that agency, he had oversight of their Bible institutes, taught courses in those institutes and worked with orphanages.

Retiring from BIEM in 2008, Dr. and Mrs. Brewer moved to Arizona. There he became the Missions Pastor at Desert Gateway Baptist Church and vice-president of Desert Baptist Bible College. His responsibilities at the college included heading up the Mission Department and the postgraduate course work. At the church he taught the Ambassador Bible class and oversaw the missions ministries. He visited missionaries on the field, and taught Bible courses during those visits. The church website says, "what a blessing for students to learn from someone who has remained steadfast in his calling despite the changes he has observed over decades of ministry involvement." Ron passed away in 2014.

Ron and Debbie (Dionysius) Brist

Student: Ron -- 1970-1975

Student: Debbie – 1976-1980

Ron Brist was led to the Lord by Bob Bardwell at Camp Clearwaters during junior high. He wrestled for Coach Hazewinkel and played soccer for Coach Bookman at Pillsbury. He worked with the youth group at Grace Baptist Church in Owatonna, under Youth Pastor John Henderson. Since graduating from Pillsbury Ron has earned his Master of Religion with an emphasis on Pastoral Counseling from Liberty Baptist Theological Seminary.

Ron's mother Erma was a sister to Pillsbury professor Dell Johnson, so Ron always called him "Uncle Dell." Since Pillsbury the Brists have worked with youth at Prior Lake Baptist Church, Southtown Baptist Church, and Berean Baptist of Burnsville. Since 2009 he has been Family and Care Pastor at Friendship Baptist Church in Prior Lake. One of the things they learned at Fourth Baptist growing up was how to run a fantastic Vacation Bible School program complete with games and exciting events for children.

Deb has worked for Bethel University and is now in the administrative offices for the Evangelical Free Church of America. The Brists have two married children, Andrew and Jynell.

David and Ardis (Hoff) Broome

Student: David --1965-1967

Student: Ardis – 1963-1966

David Broome was married to Ardis Hoff for forty-six years and four months. The Lord took her home on November 1, 2012. They served the Lord together throughout her entire life. David was a senior pastor for twenty-nine years. He served as a college professor and chaplain for three years. Then for another eight years he worked as a pastor with senior adults.

"I am 77 and headed for interim pastor training with the Interim Pastor Ministry next month," writes David. "I will probably serve the Lord Jesus in that capacity until I can't serve any more." David remarried in 2017 and lives in Cross Plains, Wisconsin. He praises the Lord for the two years God allowed him to spend at Pillsbury

Charles M. Browne

Student: 1960-1965, 1968

Charlie Browne loved photography. He used a Leica camera and would often shoot 100 feet of film per week. Many of his photographs made it into the *Northern Light* yearbook. He married Elaine Lehto in

1974. They resided in Washburn, Wisconsin, where Charlie worked various jobs.

Charlie adopted the name "Clem Kididdlehopper" from the Red Skelton show as his Facebook name and often posted pictures and memories of Pillsbury. He wrote an autobiography, *The Life and Times of Charlie Browne*, which is available from Amazon. He enjoyed freehand embroidery which he would share with family and friends. After a battle with cancer, Charlie passed away in 2018.

Larry and LaVanda (Oyloe) Brubaker

Students: 1961-1964

Larry Brubaker and LaVanda Oyloe married in the summer of 1963 and graduated the next spring. Those who knew them at Pillsbury remember how he played both the trombone and piano at the same time. They moved to Rockford, Illinois, to minister at First Baptist Church from 1964-1970. From there the Lord led them to Eagledale Baptist in Indianapolis where they worked with Warren Dafoe until 1976.

Joining the Ron Comfort Evangelistic Team in May of 1976, the Comforts and Brubakers traveled together for the next forty years, until May of 2017. In 1993 they changed their place of residence to Kings Mountain, North Carolina. When not on the road with the Comforts, they ministered at Emmanuel Baptist Church with Chuck and Rosanne Surrett. Now in retirement, they are at Emmanuel all the time.

Larry received an honorary Doctor of Music from Maranatha in 1986 and the Doctor of Divinity from Indiana Baptist College in 2008. He has published several original choir numbers as well as arrangements with Biblical Melodies. Two CDs have been produced, one of piano solos and the other of trombone solos.

Nancy Brushaber (See Nancy Sheppard)

Colene Byers (See Terry and Colene Price)

Karen Budke (See Karen Goblirsch)

Peggy (Allen) Cadwell

Student: 1962-1964

Peggy completed her training for becoming a LPN (Licensed Practical Nurse) in 1965 and married Neil Cadwell in the fall of that year. From that time on,

Peggy poured her life and soul into the work of her husband. First as a pastor's wife and then on the road in full-time evangelism, his work became the focal point of her life. They traveled from coast-to-coast in a fifth-wheel trailer. While Neil preached nightly in hundreds of churches, Peggy held children's meetings. Her storytelling brought to life a character named Herkimer who captured the imaginations of kids and introduced them to the truths of the gospel.

When they decided that their daughter, April, needed a more permanent home than the fifth-wheel, the Cadwells settled in Muncie, Indiana. Peggy was a licensed practical nurse, so she found work and April entered Christian School. Neil continued to travel, now spending much of his time overseas. The country of Ukraine became a passion. At first, there were evangelistic meetings, then the planting of churches and eventually the organization and staffing of a Bible institute to provide pastors for those churches.

Peggy made a few trips to Ukraine, but even when she wasn't traveling, she shared Neil's ministry in every way. Correspondence, scheduling, contacts, publications, letters, emails and prayer filled her schedule when he was away, caring for his health consumed her when he was home. And then, in 2017, Neil died.

What was a widow to do? Why, discover a mission field at her doorstep, of course!

The proximity to Ball State University had already brought the Cadwells into contact with some students from China. Peggy began to make those friendships even more intentional. At the beginning of the school year she watched at the Dollar Store and Walmart for people who seemed confused. An offer of help would then result in an invitation to visit in her home. Soon she was aiding foreign students to enroll their children in school, visiting Chinese homes to celebrate birthdays, and baking cookies in her kitchen with students in preparation for the Chinese New Year. Best of all, she has been holding Bible studies with various of her new friends and sharing the Gospel with all of them.

"I feel like I have moved to China," says Peggy.

Neil Cadwell

Student: 1961-1965

Neil Cadwell came to Pillsbury from Harlan, Iowa. In his biography he says he "crammed four years of college into the next five years." During that time he served as president of the European Prayer Band, never dreaming that one day he would be working in eastern Europe.

Neil served as pastor of churches in Wyoming and Kansas after graduation from Pillsbury, but his passion for evangelism soon impelled him into total dedication to that area of service. He held his first week-long evangelistic meetings in White, South Dakota, while a nineteen-year-old Pillsbury Baptist Bible College student. Itinerant evangelism soon became the pattern for life as the Cadwells moved into a fifth-wheel trailer and began traveling from church to church all across the nation.

Another change took place in 1976 when Neil held his first overseas evangelistic endeavor in Uruguay. The next fourteen years saw meetings take place not only in the United States but also in over sixty foreign countries. Souls came to know Christ through his preaching of the Word in Poland, Canada, Singapore, the West Indies, Thailand, Australia and Russia to name only a few. During those years he also returned to campus numerous times to speak in Pillsbury Chapel.

In 1990 Neil made his first trip to the former USSR and quickly fell in love with the people of Ukraine. "It was as if God did spiritual surgery in my heart," he recalls. Soon longer and longer trips to Ukraine, often four times a year, led to the establishment of the Slavic Bible Institute. Dr. Cadwell would take other men from the states with him to teach courses, and the graduates of the Institute started churches throughout the Ukrainian country-side.

By 2016 Neil had made a total of eighty-six trips to Ukraine, bringing the total distance traveled during forty years of evangelistic preaching to over two million miles. His book, *From the Cornfield to the Mission Field*, completed just before his death in 2017, summarized his ministry this way, "When we see teens with tender hearts trust Christ, sweet children placing their child-like faith in Christ, and men who know nothing but hard times and the drinking of vodka falling on their faces crying to God for forgiveness, babushkas whose eyes begin to light up with hope and tears stream down their tanned, weather-beaten, wrinkled faces when Christ lifts their heavy burdens, we shout back a hundred times over, 'It's worth it, it's worth it'."

Gail Carlson (See Paul and Gail Fosmark)

Gerald and Connie Carlson

Student: Gerald 1959-1963

President: 1994-1995

Staff: Connie 1994-1995

Gerry Carlson came to Pillsbury from the Chicago area. He graduated in 1963 and went on to Central, earning his MDiv in 1967. While there he met and married his wife Connie. At Fourth Baptist Church he worked in the youth ministry under Pastor Don Nelson.

From 1966-1970, Gerry served as Assistant Pastor in Normal, Illinois. He then became senior pastor of Faith Baptist in St. Paul, Minnesota, until 1978. The American Association of Christian Schools invited him to become their Field Director in 1978 and then later the Executive Director of that Association. He worked with them for ten years. In 1988 he became Vice-President for Administration and Development at Maranatha Baptist Bible College in Watertown, Wisconsin, and served in that position until assuming the presidency at Pillsbury in 1994.

As President, Dr. Carlson called chapel time, "The President's Classroom," and used that opportunity regularly to encourage and challenge the student body.

After leaving Pillsbury, Dr. Carlson worked in development with Positive Action for Christ, the publishers of the Pro-Teens curriculum. Because of his extensive experience and connections across the country, he excelled as a networker for that organization. Upon retirement, he and Connie moved to Maranatha Village in Sebring, Florida.

Michelle Carroll (See John and Michelle Jordan)

Jill Carter (See Jill Odens)

B. Myron Cedarholm

President: 1965-1968

Dr. B. Myron Cedarholm was born in St. Paul, Minnesota, on June 20, 1915. He married Thelma Melford in Forest Lake in 1941. Cedarholms served the pastorate of Lehigh Avenue Baptist Church in Philadelphia from 1943 to 1947 when he accepted the position as Central Area Evangelist for the newly formed Conservative Baptist Association of America. The next year he became the organization's General Director. In 1960, to honor many years of faithful service, the Conservative Baptist Churches made possible a six-month, around-the-world trip to visit 325 missionaries in 52 countries.

In 1965, Dr. Cedarholm assumed the presidency of Pillsbury Baptist Bible College. During their Pillsbury years, the Lord sent to Dr. and Mrs. Cedarholm their daughter Charlotte. Following Pillsbury, Dr. Cedarholm established Maranatha Baptist Bible College in Watertown, Wisconsin, in 1968. In 1983 Dr. Arno Q. Weniger, Jr., was named President and Cedarholm became Chancellor. The Cedarholms later moved to Clearwater, Florida, to enjoy retirement.

Dr. Cedarholm's degrees include a Bachelor of Arts from the University of Minnesota, a Bachelor of Divinity from Eastern Baptist Theological Seminary, and a Master of Theology and Doctor of Theology from Princeton. Honorary degrees were awarded by Northwestern College in Minneapolis (now University of Northwestern, St. Paul), Bob Jones University in Greenville, South Carolina, Denver Baptist Bible College in Denver, Colorado, and Maranatha Baptist University in Watertown, Wisconsin.

Dr. Cedarholm served on several ministry boards including the Fundamental Baptist Fellowship and Baptist World Mission. He is remembered as a pastor, evangelist, educator and fluent preacher of the Word of God. His life verse was Ephesians 3:20, "Now unto him that is able to do exceedingly abundantly above all that we ask or think according to the power that worketh in us." He entered the presence of the Lord on June 6, 1997 in Clearwater, Florida.

Thelma (Melford) Cedarholm

Faculty: 1965-1968

Thelma Melford trained at Gustavus Adolphus College in Minnesota, graduating in 1935 with majors in Music and English. She married Blaine Myron Cedarholm in Forest Lake, Minnesota, in 1941. Together they enrolled in Eastern Baptist Theological Seminary where she earned her Masters in Religious Education. In 1947 the Cedarholms responded to a call from the Conservative Baptist Association. Dr. Cedarholm served as General Director of the CBA while Thelma wrote church and missions materials and became a board member of the Conservative Baptist Home Mission Society. Baptist Bible College of Denver awarded her the Doctor of Literature degree in 1957. The Cedarholms adopted one daughter, Charlotte.

When Dr. Cedarholm became President of Pillsbury in 1965, Dr. Thelma Cedarholm taught Christian Education and Music. She directed the Madrigal and Handbell Choir and served as Secretary to the President. She also wrote the music for the *Pillsbury College Hymn*, with words written by Dr. Monroe Parker.

In 1968 the Cedarholms established Maranatha Baptist Bible College in Watertown, Wisconsin. Mrs. Cedarholm served as librarian and Director of

Admissions and taught Music and Christian Education. She was often in demand as a speaker for women's conferences and camps. Maranatha honored her with the Doctor of Sacred Music degree in 1988. She continued to serve as the President's secretary, directed the Madrigal and Handbell Choir and was elected to the Maranatha Board of Trustees.

On January 20, 2000, following a short illness, Mrs. Cedarholm was promoted to heaven into the presence of her deeply loved and faithfully served Lord and Savior.

Duayne and Roberta Clapp

Students: 1964-1968

Faculty: Duayne--1996-2000

Dean of Women: Roberta--1996-2000

Roberta studied at the University of Oklahoma from 1951 to 1954. From there she moved to Michigan where she met and married Duayne Clapp on February 11, 1956, in Kalamazoo. In 1964 they moved to Owatonna, Minnesota, so Duayne could attend Pillsbury and then on to Minneapolis where he enrolled at Central Baptist Theological Seminary. Together they served Calvary Baptist Church in Sheldon, Iowa, and then moved to New Ulm, Minnesota, while on deputation for the mission field.

In 1974 the Clapps left for Uruguay, South America, where they served for six years. From there the Lord led them to a nine-year ministry in Spain. In 1990 they moved again, this time to a place of service in Montreal, Canada.

1996 found the Clapps back in Owatonna where Duayne taught missions at Pillsbury and Roberta served as the Dean of Women. In 2000 it became imperative for them to care for Roberta's mother and Cheyenne, Wyoming, became home for fifteen years.

Roberta enjoyed crocheting, baking, gardening, and holding neighborhood Bible schools. She studied French and became fluent in Spanish. The Clapps have four children. Shelly and Johnnie Ashley live in Elk City, Oklahoma. Sharla and Luis Gutierrez are in Tallavera, Spain. Shawn and Penny are from Price, Utah, and Shannon and Kimberly live in Rochester, Minnesota. Roberta graduated to glory in 2017.

Shelley Beth Clapp (See Shelley Beth Ashley)

Paul and JoAnne (Pratt) Clark

Students: 1968-1972

Paul and JoAnne Clark worked in youth ministry for eight years before a summer missions trip to El Salvador, Guatemala and Columbia in 1980 changed their lives. God confirmed through those trips His missionary call for their future. They were sent to Columbia from Tulsa Baptist Temple where Paul's father Clifford Clark was the pastor.

Arriving in Bogota, they conducted home Bible studies in order to plant a church. After ten years of strong discipleship and leadership training that church numbered around 250 believers and was turned over to national leadership. They had already begun to establish new works near Bogota. Twenty-six years later there are forty churches through Columbia as well as new works in Venezuela, Peru and Madrid, Spain, all pastored by Columbian leadership. Paul's role today is to visit those works, see how they are doing, and help in any feasible way. "By God's grace we have literally lived out the Book of Acts missionary experience here in Columbia," writes Paul.

There are now more than one hundred young couples being trained for missionary service among these churches. JoAnne suffered from cancer and went to be with the Lord several years ago, but Paul says "thousands of believers in and outside of Columbia are a result of her love and dedication to the Lord and His work. Her life example has left a mark on the lives of all the believers and she is greatly missed."

Marcia (Swenson) Clay

Student: 1970-1975

Marcia has been married to Ronald Clay since December of 1975. They grew up in the same church from the time they were young and have lived on his family's farm for forty years. Both Ronald and Marcia are now retired. They vacation for three weeks each winter in Mazatlan, Mexico. Marcia says, "I love the people there and have passed out hundreds of tracts. Eternity will reveal how the Holy Spirit moved."

Marcia's main ministry has been as pianist for Calvary Baptist Church of Granada, Minnesota. She has been their pianist since she was young except for one year when she joined Grace Baptist Church in Owatonna so she could play for AWANA. "I have never received a reward for anything," writes Marcia. "I'll wait in anticipation."

Jane Clearwaters

Student: 1959-1963

Jane Clearwaters was the only child of Dr. and Mrs. Richard V. Clearwaters, the first president of Pillsbury. She was born just one year after her father began his ministry as senior pastor at Fourth Baptist Church in Minneapolis. She grew up in the church, participating in children's choir, Sunday School and the various activities of the youth group. Jane placed her faith in Christ as her Savior during a winter weekend youth retreat.

After graduation from Minnehaha Academy in 1959, Jane attended Pillsbury, graduating from there in 1963. She then took classes in psychology and completed her MA degree from St. Cloud State University. The Human Resources department of Northern States Power Company became her employer, and she worked for them for several decades. In retirement, Jane spent winters in Arizona and continued to attend Fourth Baptist Church when in the Twin Cities. She passed into the presence of the Lord on November 9, 2018.

Richard V. Clearwaters

President: 1967-1958, 1968-1975

Dr. Richard V. Clearwaters was the founder of Pillsbury Baptist Bible College. He attended Moody Bible Institute in Chicago and then Northern Baptist Theological Seminary where he graduated with the ThB and BD degrees in 1928. From there he earned a scholarship to Kalamazoo College in Kalamazoo, Michigan, and graduated with a BA degree in 1929. He was a few hours short of a PhD when time and money became prohibitive. In addition, Clearwaters held three honorary doctorate degrees.

When he moved to Kalamazoo he pastored the First Baptist Church of Lawton for nine months and then Bethel Baptist Church of Kalamazoo. While at Bethel he met a registered nurse named Florence Welch who

58

worked for the city Health Department. They were engaged but waited a year to marry due to the challenging times of the Depression and busy schedules. Florence became Mrs. Richard Clearwaters on April 17, 1935.

When he was done with school, Richard began to look for a permanent pastorate. Cedar Rapids, Iowa, called and they ministered there for four and one-half years, preaching the Gospel and doing evangelism. Clearwaters was soon elected President of the Iowa Baptist State Convention. In 1939 the pulpit committee of the Fourth Baptist Church of Minneapolis contacted Pastor Clearwaters. They accepted the church's call and moved to Minneapolis on January 1, 1940. Dr. Clearwaters pastored Fourth until his retirement in 1982.

Fourth Baptist is a member of the Minnesota Baptist Association, which in 1940 was an adjunct of the Northern Baptist Convention, later to become the American Baptist Convention. By the 1940s, due to growing concerns of liberalism, a group of fundamentalists, including W. B. Riley, had organized a Fundamental Fellowship within the national convention. In 1943, the Conservative Baptist Association of America was formed with Dr. R. V. Clearwaters as its first President and Dr. B. Myron Cedarholm as its General Director.

During these years Clearwaters also served as a trustee of the Northwestern Theological Seminary in Minneapolis which had been founded by W. B. Riley, pastor of First Baptist Church. Clearwaters and Riley had a close relationship until Riley's death in 1947. In 1956 Northwestern discontinued the Seminary and Bible College, combining them into Northwestern

College. Clearwaters felt the continued need for a fundamental seminary and organized Central Baptist Theological Seminary in 1956. Then Clearwaters led the court fight which reclaimed the Pillsbury Academy campus from the liberal side of the Convention and founded a four-year "Biblical Arts" college in Owatonna. In 1957, the Minnesota Supreme Court ruled that the Minnesota Baptist Association could choose the trustees and officers of the school. Dr. Clearwaters became the first President of the college. He resumed that role after Dr. Cedarholm left and for the first five years after Dr. Rammel came.

As pastor of Fourth Baptist Church, Clearwaters continued to build a large church with a broad ministry. A Bible Institute was added in 1958, Camp Clearwaters in 1963, an FM radio station in 1965, a Christian school in 1966, and in 1973 a 2400 seat auditorium at the Broadway Street location.

Dr. Clearwaters retired as pastor of Fourth Baptist Church and became President Emeritus of Pillsbury Baptist Bible College in 1982. He retired as President of Central Baptist Seminary in 1987. Florence preceded him in death in 1989 and "Doc" went home to be with the Lord on September 30, 1996.

Dave Coats

Student: 1975-1979

After graduation Dave moved to Minneapolis to attend Central Seminary. He graduated in 1982 and the Coats family went on deputation, planning ministry in the island of Haiti. In the fall of 1983 they arrived in Port-au-Prince. Life in a third world country was challenging, but they loved the ministry to Haitians and to Arabic people-groups. God taught them immense lessons through various trials including a government takeover in 1986.

The government was again in turmoil in 1990, and through much prayer Dave and Judith felt it necessary to leave Haiti. They moved to New Brunswick, Canada, where Dave became assistant pastor to Pillsbury alumnus Paul Fosmark. They worked with the youth and started a camp called Windcrest Bible Camp.

In 1996 God called them to Northland International University where Dave served for many years as Dean of Men. They started a community youth center in Pembine, Wisconsin, which helped open a community to the needs of children and youth. He also pastored Dunbar Community Bible Church from 2008-2018. In

2018 the family moved to Littleton, Colorado, to serve in the church body of Sola Church.

Dr. Coats received a doctoral degree from Central Seminary in 2006. He has authored a book called *Soul Purity*, and co-authored *Help! My Teen is Rebellious!* with his wife Judith.

Judith (Sand) Coats

Student: 1976-1980

Judith Coats taught English for one year at Grace Baptist Christian School in Owatonna and then high school English at Fourth Baptist Christian School while Dave finished seminary. Their daughter Julie was born in Minneapolis. In 1983 they arrived in Port-au-Prince, Haiti, as missionaries. Two more children, Jennifer and Jonathan were born in Haiti.

Dave and Judith consider it a great blessing that all three of their children have married godly spouses. They have eight grandchildren and enjoy the growth in the Gospel they have learned from interaction with their married children.

When it became necessary to leave Haiti in 1990, the Coats family moved to New Brunswick, Canada, to work with Rev. Paul Fosmark. There they started a camp called Windcrest Bible Camp. When they were called to Northland International University, Judith taught English. She served as the English Department Chair from 2003 to 2015 when Northland closed.

Dr. Judith Coats completed her doctoral degree from Regent University in Virginia Beach, Virginia, in 2012.

She co-authored *Help! My Teen is Rebellious!* with her husband Dave. She has also written *Choosing Wisdom: Solomon's Proverbs Reclaimed,* and *A Sentence Diagramming Primer,* as well as a book following the life of Dr. Les Ollila titled *A Man Among Them.*

Vicki Coats (See Kenneth and Vicki Mansell)

John Colyer

Faculty: 1987-1990

John Colyer completed his undergraduate education at Cedarville College in Ohio and Baptist Bible College in Pennsylvania. Seminary training came from Tennessee Temple University and Calvary Baptist Seminary where he earned his MDiv. He came to teach at Pillsbury in 1987 after years of successful youth ministry at High Point Camp, Calvary Baptist Church of Lansdale, Pennsylvania, and Calvary Baptist Church of Lancaster, Pennsylvania.

Colyer taught Church Ministry and Christian Education courses at Pillsbury and also served as Dean of Students. He started Camp Shiloh at a campground near Ortonville, Minnesota. After Pillsbury he taught at Faith Baptist Bible College in Ankeny, Iowa, served as Christian Education Pastor at Grace Church in Des Moines and then became pastor of Ankeny Free Church.

John loved young people and he loved missions. He made numerous trips to Zambia where he taught at International Bible College. He was known for his zeal, his contagious laughter and his desire to make himself available as a mentor to countless young men. In 2015 John went to be with the Lord while on a missions trip to Lusaka, Zambia. He and Judie had enjoyed forty-two years together. In additional to their four sons, God gave them eight grandsons and one granddaughter. The night before he left for Zambia he had held his grandson Bo for the first time.

Peggy Cooper (See John and Peggy Katsion)

Jeff Coyle

Student: 1987-1992

Jeff Coyle taught fifth grade at Chapel Christian Academy in Limerick, Pennsylvania, until 2006. God has given the Coyles seven children. "I love seeing my children serving the Lord through music in our church and anywhere else God opens a door," writes Jeff. "I wish I would have taken advantage of those opportunities in college."

Since 2006 Jeff has been the Logistics Director for a Christian company called Buckman's. According to the website Buckman's Inc. is "the East Coast leading water treatment chemical supplier and distributor, ice melt supplier and distributor and swimming pool chemical supplier and distributor."

Dawn Craig (See Dawn Musson)

Robert Crane

President: 1996-2008

Before being called into the ministry, Robert Crane had been a welding engineer. He attended LeTourneau College and then worked in manufacturing for the R. G. LeTourneau Company. He was also a United States Marine and would often use illustrations from his military days in his sermons.

Dr. Crane completed his MDiv at Central in 1974 and attended International Baptist Seminary in Chandler, Arizona. Prior to his presidency at Pillsbury, he served pastorates in Detroit Lakes, Farmington, and International Falls, Minnesota. He had a genuine love for the disabled and promoted an active "Friends" ministry in International Falls. He also reached out to the First Nations (American Indian) people and developed in the church a passion for missions with a particular interest in sharing Christ with Muslims.

When he arrived on campus in 1996, Dr. Crane initiated several practices to strengthen academics and unify the campus. All-night prayer meetings called "Nights on our Knees" were started. The ministry to deaf students developed under his presidency. Widespread use of the internet was just in its infancy, and Randy Miller remembers working with President Crane to provide email and internet access for all the student body.

The 2001 Northern Light Yearbook was dedicated to Dr. Crane. When he retired in 2008 he became Pillsbury's second President Emeritus, the first being the college's founder Dr. R. V. Clearwaters. Since retirement, Dr. Crane has been the Director of Ministerial Advancement at Rio Grande Bible College in Edinburg, Texas. There he travels to make friends for the school, and does financial planning including writing wills, trusts and gift annuities.

Tammy (Allen) Cress

Student: 1995-1996

Tammy Allen transferred to Baptist Bible College of Clarks Summit, Pennsylvania, and graduated with a BS in Counseling in 1999. She married Paul Cress in 2001 and lives in Lancaster County, Pennsylvania. They have three children, Bryan, Hannah and AJ.

For the past twenty years Tammy has had the privilege of working with the drama ministry of Cocalico Community Church in Denver, Pennsylvania and then Christian Fellowship Church in New Holland. She writes and directs monthly dramatic scripts and occasional full-length productions. For several years she participated in yearly Purity Camps sponsored by First Baptist Church of Maxwell, Nebraska, and wrote the skits used during that time as well as leading and counseling campers.

In 2014 Tammy and her husband Paul decided to home-school their children. "This is at once both the most challenging and most rewarding endeavor I have ever undertaken," writes Tammy, "but God has proved himself faithful in our lives over and over again. My greatest victories have always come through seeing my children grow in grace and in the knowledge of their Lord and Savior Jesus Christ."

John Crivea

Faculty: 1978-1984

During the eighties Pillsbury expanded into some professional ministry training areas including industrial arts. John Crivea came to Owatonna to teach in that department. He was a graduate of Oakland Community College. During his years on faculty he completed his degree in Bible from Pillsbury.

John grew interested in construction at the age of twelve and over the years built homes, churches, Christian campgrounds and commercial buildings. He also served in the U.S. Army National Guard from 1955-1962. He constantly shared the Gospel of Jesus Christ on construction mission teams, while working for churches and colleges and on his own personal time. He lived the Gospel before his children and spoke of it often to his grandchildren and great-grandchildren.

In addition to teaching at Pillsbury, John taught Advanced Math at Oakland Community College and Construction, Math and Mechanical Systems at the School of Applied Studies at Bob Jones University.

John died in White Lake, Michigan on May 17, 2017.

Lori Cross (See Lori Moffitt)

Bob Cundiff

Student: 1963-1967

Faculty: 1969-1971, 1976-1981

Bob graduated from both Pillsbury and Central as well as earning his PhD from Southern Illinois University in Carbondale, Illinois. He served as Speech Department Chair at Pillsbury from 1976-1981 and as Communications Arts Department Chair and professor at Clearwater Christian College in Clearwater, Florida, for nineteen years. He married Kirsten Eastergard of Copenhagen, Denmark, who died in 2013 after forty-three years of marriage.

Bob has been a radio host, producer of out-door theatre in southern Illinois, and has recorded voice-overs for more than 800 commercials. He has served as an adjunct faculty member at St. Petersburg College for twenty years. Cundiff is the author of one published and three produced stage plays and a member of the Dramatists Guild.

Dr. Cundiff is a member of the Clearwater City Council in Clearwater, Florida. He is past-president of the Sons of the American Revolution, Clearwater Chapter, and a member of Gideons International. He is a member of Lakeside Community Chapel and does volunteer work through the church, including a ministry to homeless veterans. Bob enjoys photography, playwriting, ballroom dancing, biking and swimming.

Lillian Cundiff

Staff: 1967-1987

Lillian Mazzi married Stanley Cundiff and had two children, Judith and Robert. They lived in Winchester, Virginia, during WWII. Stanly worked for Gulf Oil Corporation there and later in Allentown, Pennsylvania.

69

He died of a heart attack at age 44 while serving as a camp counselor in LeTourneau Christian Camp in Canandaigua, New York.

Trained as a secretary and bookkeeper, Lillian had been working at the First Baptist Church of Allentown. In 1959 she moved to Minneapolis to become secretary at the Minnesota Baptist Convention headquarters on Blaisdell Avenue. The family attended Fourth Baptist Church. She worked for a brief time at Honeywell, and then, in 1967 moved to Owatonna to be the bookkeeper at Pillsbury. Later she became the financial office manager. The 1986 Pillsbury Northern Light yearbook was dedicated to her.

Upon retirement, she moved to New Jersey to live with Judy. She had decided to find part-time employment, but on the day she was to interview, she had a heart attack while driving. Miraculously, she survived the accident, had bypass surgery and recovered. She moved with her daughter to New York where her health declined after several years and she passed into glory in 1996. Lillian was a humble, faithful servant of the Lord. The gifts she had, she gave to the Lord for His work.

Ed Cunningham

Student: 1966-1970

Staff Photographer: 1974-1995

Ed Cunningham came to Pillsbury from Tulsa Baptist Temple in Tulsa, Oklahoma. When he received his draft notice in 1970 he entered the Army. He had married his wife Shirlee and they were expecting their first child. During basic training he was sent to Army photography school and then served as White House photographer during the Nixon era from 1971-1974.

In the midst of the Watergate scandal, Dr. Joseph Rammel offered Ed a chance to start a photography department at Pillsbury. Things weren't looking well for President Nixon who resigned on August 8, 1974. Ed left on August 9 for Owatonna. "I tell people that when he was thoroughly convinced I was leaving, he decided to quit as well," Ed often jokes.

The photo lab was set up in the basement of Old Main. Ed finished his Pillsbury degree and then earned a master's from Mankato State. In addition to teaching photography he was the golf coach. A highlight of each year was the annual Photo Banquet where he showed his appreciation for all the people who helped take and develop photos and kept the lab running smoothly. He also ran a personal business, Edward S. Cunningham Photography, doing weddings and commercial photography.

When the photography program was discontinued in 1995, Ed took a job with Child Evangelism Fellowship as the editor of their magazine. The Cunninghams later moved back to Owatonna. Ed worked for a monument company, utilizing his graphic skills, and currently works for Cabela's.

Joe and Wendy (Allen) Daniels

Student: Joe – 1993-1996

Student: Wendy – 1990-1994

Joe and Wendy Daniels moved from Owatonna to Grand Rapids, Michigan, where Joe completed work for his master's degree from Grand Rapids Theological Seminary. They spent twelve years in ministry in churches in Pennsylvania, Florida and Michigan where Joe served as associate pastor and then lead pastor. Since 2013 they have lived in the Atlanta, Georgia, area where Joe works with his father. He coaches girl's high school basketball at Trinity Christian School. Wendy directs a children's choir and serves on the worship team at New Hope Baptist Church.

The Daniels have seen the faithfulness of God demonstrated in their lives and know that He will be there for the future as well. Each experience has been used of God to prepare them for what He has next. They know that just as He has been faithful to them, so He will be for their three children as they go through life.

Stephen and Diane (Beenken) Davis

Student: Stephen – 1976-1981

Student: Diane – 1974-1979

Diane Beenken completed her degree in Elementary Education from Pillsbury in 1978 and began teaching first grade at Faith Baptist Christian School in St. Paul, Minnesota. She taught there until 1987.

Stephen Davis graduated from Pillsbury in 1981 and began work on his MDiv at Central the same year. He worked for WCTS FM from 1981-1987 when he graduated from Central Seminary.

Diane and Stephen were married July 25, 1987. Stephen accepted the position of Assistant Pastor at Adelphi Calvary Baptist Church in Runnells, Iowa, where he served from 1987-1988. He was then called to Grace Baptist Church of Cherokee, Iowa, as Senior Pastor and worked in that ministry until 1998.

WCTS FM invited Stephen back to Plymouth in 1998 as Operations Manager. In 2011 he became the General Manager of the station and continues to serve in that capacity. Diane taught first grade at Faith Baptist Christian School until 2001 and then began teaching second grade at Fourth Baptist Christian School where she continues to teach today. Stephen and Diane have one son, Benjamin who married Tatiana Bespolava in

Yaraslavl, Russia, in 2017. They live near Benjamin and his wife in Plymouth, Minnesota.

Michelle Deckert (See Rich and Michelle Harris)

Wayne and Ruth Deckert

Staff: Ruth – 1967-1996

Faculty: Wayne – 1967-1996

Wayne Deckert headed up the Science Department and coached a variety of sports for almost thirty years at Pillsbury. Ruth worked in the bookstore. They enjoyed the opportunity of influencing young people for Christ as well as the privilege of raising their three children, Greg, Michelle, and Scott in a small-town, godly environment.

From Pillsbury the Deckerts moved to Clearwater, Florida. At Clearwater Christian College Wayne taught Biology, Biochemistry, and Genetics as well as offering Field Biology in summer courses. Ruth managed the college bookstore.

Upon retirement in 2008 they built a home in Rochester, Minnesota, to be near their grandchildren. Wayne has taught and coached part-time at Schaeffer Academy since then. It has been their greatest blessing to see their children active in local churches and raising their families to serve the Lord. The Deckerts are active at Cornerstone Baptist Church in Pine Island, Minnesota.

Paul Dilger

Staff: 1989-1991

Paul Dilger accepted the Lord as a fourteen-year-old camper at Word of Life Island in Schroon Lake, New York. He studied at the University of Massachusetts and graduated from the Culinary Institute of America in 1965. Paul and his wife Jeanie met at Mt. McKinley National Park in Anchorage, Alaska, and were married in 1970.

Paul worked as a professional chef for various Christian organizations including conference centers, camps and colleges. His ministry took him many places including Des Moines, Iowa, Plympton, Massachusetts, Schroon Lake, New York, Owatonna, Minnesota, Estes Park, Colorado, and Kodak, Tennessee. He supported missionaries worldwide and spent countless hours praying for and encouraging others. He also enjoyed gardening, yard sales, giving gifts and visiting friends.

As a member of First Baptist Church, Sevierville, Tennessee, Paul was active in the CARE ministry. He went to be with the Lord on September 21, 2015.

Debbie Dionysius (See Ron and Debbie Brist)

Carol (Sailors) Dobson

Student: 1971-1975

Faculty: 1975-1976

Carol Sailors married Steve Dobson and they stayed in Owatonna for more than forty years. She served as pianist at Grace Baptist Church and taught piano while raising their sons Brian and Scott. In 2001 the Dobsons opened a Coffee Shop on North Cedar where they sold Espresso Drinks Coffee, Kustom Katerers famous caramel and cinnamon rolls, and did catering. Several students from Pillsbury worked for them part-time during those years.

Steve and Carol started a Free Food for the Needy while at the Coffee Shop. Every Thursday they served those from the community with financial problems and emotional needs. Carol also returned to school and completed two additional degrees, an MDiv and a Masters in Marriage and Family Therapy from Bethel University.

When Steve was diagnosed with Parkinson's in 2015 the Dobsons moved to Maple Grove, Minnesota. Their son Brian prepared an apartment for them in the basement of his house. There Carol started a Marriage and Family Therapy practice.

Steve Dobson

Student:1971-1976

Faculty: 1990-1991

Steve began working for Truth Hardware while a student at Pillsbury and stayed with them for eighteen years. He married Carol Sailors before his final year in college. In 1989 he graduated from the University of St. Thomas with an MBA and left Truth to start ITI Seminar and Consulting. He also worked at Enderes Tools as a plant manager in Albert Lea and then SPX PowerTeam as the Training Manager. When PowerTeam moved to Illinois they decided to stay in Owatonna and purchased Kustom Katerers. They opened their Coffee Shop in 2001 and ran that until 2006 when Steve went to work for Lowes. During the time at the Coffee Shop he says that God taught him patience and perseverance, trusting Him to meet their financial needs.

At Grace Baptist Church Steve taught Sunday School, served as Sunday School Superintendent, Deacon, and member of the Christian School Board. He taught classes at St. Mary's Graduate College, Crown College and various Technical Community Colleges as well as seminars. His interest in theatre led to involvement in numerous plays at Little Theatre of Owatonna. Steve developed a class on the DiSC personality assessment called "Understanding Self and Others."

In 2015 Steve was diagnosed with Parkinson's and they moved to Maple Grove, Minnesota, to an apartment on the lower level of their son Brian's home. Steve accepted a part-time position as a Barista at Dunn Brother's Coffee. He dearly misses teaching and has plans in his retirement years to dust off some of the courses he taught and start another company.

Loren and Jeanne "Jean" Douglas

Students: 1960-1964

Loren and Jean Douglas arrived in Owatonna with three children in 1960. After graduation they moved to Minneapolis to attend Central with five children. Eventually God gave them a total of seven. Together they served churches in Lake Lillian, Minnesota, and Oak Lawn, Illinois, and then Loren taught school and served as associate to Dr. Wayne Van Geldren.

In 1973 the Douglas family moved to Havre, Montana, to pastor and start the High Line Christian School. Jean served as secretary and they both taught in the school. They became involved in the work at Castle Rock Baptist Camp. Loren did electrical work at the camp and laid the foundations for several cabins and the Allen Lodge.

In order to keep the children in Christian schools, the Douglas family moved to Cody, Wyoming, and then to Minneapolis. Loren worked on the MRE degree at Central Baptist Seminary. In 1988 God called them to Faith Baptist Church of Wisconsin Rapids. Health issues necessitated a return to Minneapolis in 1992. Since that time, they have been active at Berean Baptist Church.

Loren and Jean consider it the greatest thrill of their lives to see their family, now numbering sixty-four, serving God. A gospel tape *The Douglas Family Singers* has been a blessing to many.

Gloria Dreyer (See Gloria Taylor)

Gordon Edgington

Student: 1960-1963

Gordon Edgington was called to active service with the United States Army Air Force in 1945 and spent nineteen months on Guam-Mariana Island in the South Pacific Theatre of Operation. He married Lois Maxine Schofield in 1948.

The Edgingtons moved to Owatonna where Gordon attended Pillsbury. He was ordained to the ministry on May 21, 1965. He received a Doctor of Divinity degree in 1979 from Indiana Baptist College in Indianapolis, Indiana.

Dr. Edgington pastored churches in Fremont, Nebraska, and Oak Lawn, Illinois. He served as the Missions Director of the Association of Independent Baptist Churches of Illinois for twenty-four years. He and his wife traveled over one million miles in the state of Illinois, ministering to churches and starting eight new works. The association started a total of twenty-four new churches during those years.

Dr. Gordon Edgington passed away on Friday, December 14, 2018 at the Illiana Veterans Affairs Hospital in Danville, Illinois. He was buried with military rites accorded by the American Legion Post 210.

Roger Edmonds

Student: 1972

Roger Edmonds attended Moody Bible Institute in Chicago where he met and married Patricia Fredrickson in 1961. He became Minister of Youth at First Baptist Church of Rochelle, Illinois, and the Edmonds were blessed with the birth of their two sons while serving there. He continued his education at Pillsbury, graduating in 1972, and then Central Seminary where he graduated in 1976.

The Edmonds served three pastorates in Minnesota as part of the Minnesota Baptist Association, working as church planters. Immediately after seminary they moved to Farmington, Minnesota. Then they spent ten years in Red Wing, and eleven years in Tyler before moving to Redwood Falls in 2001. Roger went to be with Lord in 2018.

Elaine Eggerth (See Paul and Elaine Rudy)

Robert and Elfrieda "Fritz" Eiseman

Faculty: Robert – 1969-1987

Staff: Elfrieda – 1969-1987

Bob Eiseman served in various roles while at Pillsbury. He was Chairman of the Mathematics Department, Registrar, Athletic Director, Director of Teacher Placement and Head of Maintenance. He also coached a variety of different sports. His wife, Elfrieda (Fritz) was the switchboard receptionist. They had three children, Dana, Roberta and Robin. He received a Master's in Educational Administration from Mankato State.

When their daughter Robin died in 1995, the Eisemans established an Owatonna Park and Recreation Scholarship in her memory. The fund aided children who couldn't afford to participate in summer Park and Rec activities.

After leaving Pillsbury, Robert became the administrator at Berean Christian School in Rockford, Illinois. Upon retirement they returned to Owatonna where he remained active as the Athletic Director at Owatonna Junior High and ran the Kids First program through Owatonna Park and Rec. He passed away after suffering a heart attack while attending a great-grandchild's sporting event in 2014.

Jonathan Engen

Student: 1973-1977

Jonathan Engen did not want to attend Pillsbury. He wanted to go to radio school and get lost in the world of microphones, audio tape and transmitters. He remembers Dr. Clearwaters saying that when God calls, He also calls to prepare. Pillsbury had to come first, and since then he has stepped behind a mic with the theology and Biblical knowledge learned at Pillsbury coming out of his mouth.

Jon says that he watched *Never the Same* to prepare for filling out his questionnaire. He watched a very young Jon Engen singing in that film with no idea of what things would look like forty years later. The Engens now have two "amazing" children who married equally "amazing" people, and three grandsons.

Engen has spent his life in Christian Radio. He worked for Northwestern College Radio for twenty-three years, finishing there as Manager of KTIS. He now works for KAXL in Bakersfield, California. Travels for the station have taken him to Greece, Italy, Turkey and Israel. He has served as a board member for the National Religious Broadcasters and represented the International Council of Broadcasters for a time. In 1997 he stepped into the host position for The Haven of Rest Ministries. During his years on radio he earned an MDiv and served for seventeen years as a bi-vocational senior pastor.

Jon is now in school again working on a Masters in Adolescent Psychology with an emphasis on the reasons for and prevention of suicide. "I know that what Pillsbury gave me was successful in laying a solid foundation," he writes.

Lynda (Grantham) England

Student: 1981-1985

After graduation Lynda returned to Ordway, Colorado, to teach in the ACE Christian school she had attended during junior high and high school. She married Doug England in 1986. They worked together in Colorado and then in the Bible Baptist Christian School in Missoula, Montana, where Pillsbury graduate Marcus Moffitt was the pastor. In 1991 Doug became a youth pastor in Arvada, Colorado, and three years later they returned to Montana where they served a church in Dillon. For the past several years they have lived in Colorado, raising and home- schooling five children.

One of Lynda's greatest blessings has been raising the five amazing children God has entrusted to her and her husband. It has been an immense joy to watch them grow, learn and make decisions by looking to God for guidance and peace. Doug has faced serious heart issues for several years and she gives God all the praise for allowing her husband to still be with them. They are part of a Bible-believing church where they can fellowship with God-loving, God-fearing friends. Doug teaches Sunday School and Lynda is involved in music and the children's ministry.

Wayne Erickson

Student: 1989

Wayne Erickson married his wife Margie in 1976 and they have six grown children all of whom attended and graduated from Lake Region Christian School in Baxter, Minnesota. The Ericksons served as foster parents in Crow Wing County, caring for twenty-four children over the span of nine years. They owned and operated their own restaurant for over twenty years before going into the ministry.

Wayne attended Pillsbury and has taken classes from Liberty University as well as Biblical Counseling training in Lafayette, Indiana. He has been Assistant Pastor at First Baptist Church in Baxter since 2005, working with Pastor Dave Grotzke. His responsibilities include Sunday School, Kid's Bible Club and hospitality. He also serves as a Lake Region Christian School advisor and oversees the building and grounds.

Dale Evans (See Dale J. Moe)

David H. Farrington

Board of Trustees: 1957 - 1972

Dr. David H. Farrington was a member of the Pillsbury Academy Board before the Bible college ever came into existence. He was appointed by the judge as the point man during the time when the Minnesota Baptist Convention was seeking to change the Academy into a Bible College. That meant that nothing could be changed without his approval during the time when the previous board was disbanded and the Pillsbury Baptist Bible College board assumed ownership. Dr. Farrington continued as vice-president of the Pillsbury Board for many years. He pastored in Blooming Prairie, just seventeen miles south of Owatonna.

Dorothy Farrington (See Dorothy Kettlewell)

Darlene (Lane) Fish

Student: 1972-1976

Darlene had only been saved for one year before enrolling at Pillsbury in 1972. Pillsbury became her spiritual home and provided her the grounding she needed in His Word. When she left for college her parents told her not to become fanatical, but at her graduation they told Dr. Rammel they wanted to send another of their children to study there.

After graduation Darlene taught at Calvary Baptist Christian School in Lancaster, Pennsylvania, from 1976-1983. She married Mark Fish in 1982 and God gave them four children, David, Stacey, Sarah and Eric. All four of the children attended Pillsbury as well.

In 1990 God called Mark to become the pastor of First Baptist Church of Lake Benton, Minnesota, a rural community of 693 people. They stayed in that pastorate for the next twenty-three years. Together they raised their children and home-schooled them. Darlene served as a Sunday School teacher, taught in Vacation Bible School, worked in Ladies Bible studies and Junior church. She also became involved in the community, getting to know people through a side business of antiques. In 2003 they purchased an established antique mall in Brookings, South Dakota, which they still own and run.

Darlene's goal has been to be faithful in serving Jesus Christ and using what He has given her for Him. When Mark resigned from the pastorate in 2013 they both agreed that they should stay in Lake Benton. They had built contacts which would take another man years to build and by staying in town they could be a blessing to the church, the community and the new pastor. Darlene says, "I try not to dwell on what I have done, but to keep doing."

Mark Fish

Student: 1977-1981

After graduation, Mark enrolled at Calvary Baptist Seminary in Lansdale, Pennsylvania. He and his new bride, Darlene (married in 1982) decided to live in Lancaster from where Mark would commute. They knew it would be a sacrifice of time and driving for Mark to make the 144-mile round trip to attend classes, but they both wanted to stay and serve actively at Calvary Baptist Church of Lancaster. Mark completed his MDiv in 1986.

The First Baptist Church of Lake Benton, Minnesota, called Mark to be their pastor in 1990. Moving from a much larger town in Pennsylvania to the rural community of Lake Benton seemed like a real change, but God gave him peace about the call. He continued to serve as pastor in Lake Benton for the next twenty-three years.

In Lake Benton, he and Darlene raised their four children, David, Stacey, Sarah and Eric. They home-schooled and kept active in the church and community. All four children attended Pillsbury and three of them graduated from there.

When Mark decided to retire from the church in 2013, he believed that he should continue to serve in the community even though he was not pastoring the church. He and Darlene had made many contacts over the years, to the place that many in town thought they grew up there. A number of unsaved people had invited him to perform funerals simply because they had come to know him well and respected what he stood for. His desire is to continue working in the community and church, alongside the new pastor, to the glory of God.

Gerald Fisher

Student: 1966-1971

Gerald Fisher has been the pastor of the Bible Baptist Church of Crosby, Minnesota, for forty years and continues to serve in that position at the present time. After graduation from Pillsbury he enrolled at Central Baptist Seminary. Pastor Kenneth Dobson from Leadville, Colorado, invited him to join the staff of the "highest Baptist church in America" as assistant pastor. Fishers stayed in Leadville until 1978 when he was called to become the senior pastor in Crosby.

Maxine (Nelson) Fisher

Student: 1967-1971

Maxine married Gerald Fisher in 1969. After Pillsbury they moved to Minneapolis where Gerald attended Central Baptist Theological Seminary. Three and a half years were spent in Colorado where he served as assistant pastor in Leadville before moving to Crosby, Minnesota. The Fishers have ministered at the Bible Baptist Church of Crosby since 1978.

Gerald and Maxine are the parents of four children. She worked as a classroom assistant for three years and then home-schooled their own four. She has been a tremendous help in the church, particularly in the areas of Sunday School teaching and Junior church.

Deborah Fitzgerald (See Jay and Deborah Richerson)

Dennis and Sharon (Hartsock) Fitzgerald

Student: Dennis – 1960-1968

Student: Sharon – 1960-1961, 1967-1968

Board Member: 2000-2008

Dennis Fitzgerald served as youth pastor in Oakland, Minnesota, during his college years, from 1962-1968. From there the Fitzgeralds moved to Milltown, Wisconsin, where Dennis became youth pastor at the First Baptist Church, serving in that position until 1975. The Elmwood Baptist Church of Elmwood, Illinois, called him as senior pastor in 1975 and he served there until his retirement in 2017.

God has given the Fitzgeralds three children, eleven grandchildren and six great grandchildren. He earned his Master of Ministry degree from Northland Baptist Bible College in 1993. Pillsbury recognized his service with an Alumni Citation in 1989. Dennis has served on the boards of the Faith Baptist Mission and the Slavic Baptist Mission. He was a member of the board of the Association of Independent Baptist Churches of Illinois from 1980-2016. Sharon served as treasurer of the Ladies AIBCI Board from 1986-1990.

Larry G. Forsberg

Student: 1967-1971

Larry Forsberg married Joanne Sundstrom in 1972 and graduated from Central Seminary in 1974 with an MDiv. Degree. He enjoyed thirty years of pastoral ministry including serving as youth pastor in Pekin, Illinois, senior pastor of Holmes Baptist Church, associate pastor of Valley Baptist in Golden Valley, Minnesota, senior pastor of First Baptist in Bloomington, associate pastor of Grace Baptist in Napa, California, and senior pastor of Oakridge Church in Stillwater, Minnesota. From 2004 to 2006 he served with the Missions to Sports program and then became a Prison Fellowship Director. From 2008 to the present time Larry serves as lead Chaplain at Boutwills Landing, Stillwater.

During his time as a youth pastor Larry helped start Faith Bible Institute in Pekin, Illinois. Several of the churches he served enjoyed remodels and plant expansions during his ministry including Holmes Baptist, Valley Baptist, Grace in Napa and Oakridge. They started the Fellowship of Christian Athletes endorsed program called True Sports Baseball in 1991. Through that program they have encouraged competitive baseball church outreach in Minnesota and Texas, serving more than 300 children in youth baseball every summer.

Paul and Gail (Carlson) Fosmark

Student: Paul -- 1960-1965 (Graduated in 1964 and took graduate work in 1965)

Student: Gail -- 1961-1963

Gail Carlson graduated from Mankato State with a BS in Elementary Education in December of 1965. She married Paul Fosmark on December 21 of that year. Paul served as youth pastor and music director at Grace Baptist Church in Owatonna during his college years. From Owatonna the Fosmarks moved to Minneapolis where Paul attended Central Seminary, graduating in 1972.

At Fourth Baptist Church in Minneapolis, Paul served as Senior Youth Pastor from 1966 -1982. He taught at Central from 1972-1982, working with Dr. R. V. Clearwaters for a total of sixteen years. The youth pastorate involved an extensive camp ministry at Camp Clearwaters, many youth trips and the popular and exciting "Singspirations" which attracted youth from across the Twin Cities after services on Sunday nights.

In 1982 Paul accepted the call to become pastor of Fundamental Baptist Church in Saint John, New Brunswick, Canada. He served as interim pastor at Bethel Baptist Church in Minto, New Brunswick from 1998-2001 and then pastored Jones Lake Baptist Church in Moncton from 2002-2017. Retiring to a wonderful farm in the New Brunswick countryside in 2017, the Fosmarks immediately started working on planting an independent Baptist Church in a farming community called Steeves Settlement.

Paul has presented workshops on "The Perils of Rock Music," and "Youth Work versus Christian Day

Schools." He rejoices in the fact that he is still a convicted Baptist, fundamentalist, separatist, local church man. Highlights of ministry have included starting a youth camp as well as founding and teaching in two Bible Institutes. God has given Paul and Gail a son, Andy, and a daughter Sara as well as three terrific grandchildren, Wes, Wil and Skye.

Donald and Peggy (Neuenschwander) Fowler

Student: Don --1963-1967

Student: Peggy – 1963-1967

Following graduation from Pillsbury, Don Fowler earned his MDiv, a ThM in Hebrew and Old Testament, and a ThD in Hebrew and Old Testament from Grace Theological Seminary in Winona, Lake, Indiana. He has served three full-time pastorates as wells as nineteen interim pastorates. Dr. Fowler has spoken as a guest lecturer in numerous colleges. He taught for twenty years at Grace Seminary and has been on the faculty at Liberty University for an additional twenty years.

During his years at Liberty University, Don has also taught occasional classes at Liberty Baptist Theological Seminary. He has published frequently in books and encyclopedias and served for twelve years as the book review editor of the Grace Theological Journal. He presently serves as a professor in the School of Divinity for Liberty University of Lynchburg, Virginia.

Russell Frederick

Student: 1959-1962

Russell Frederick attended Central after graduation and completed work there in 1966. He was ordained the same year. He and his wife, Mary Lou Hippauf, were married in 1965, and God has given them three children, Valeri Hornor, Sonia Petereit and Heidi Maute. They also have eight grandchildren.

The Fredericks were appointed as missionaries to Germany by Baptist World Mission and arrived on the field in 1968. They served for forty-one years and started New Testament churches in three different cities with many souls saved and growing in the Lord.

During seminary, Russ served with Gus Carns in a Fourth Baptist mission church called Sumner Baptist, helping in the youth ministry. He was also a member of

Woodcrest Baptist Church in Fridley for a time under the ministry of Dr. Ernest Pickering.

Their three girls grew up in Germany, and both Sonia and Heidi married Germans and continue to live and work in that country. Russ and Mary's children attended Northland Baptist Bible College in Dunbar, Wisconsin, which is where Valerie met her husband, David Hornor.

In addition to the church work and student ministries in Germany, Russ was blessed to travel behind the Iron Curtain with fellow Pillsbury graduate Gene Mumford. They conducted preaching services and taught with help from translators in East Germany, Poland and Czechoslovakia.

Arnie Fredricks

Student: 1967-1971

Even as a young boy working on a farm in Southwestern Minnesota, Arnie remembered having trouble seeing in the evening hours. When he entered the service, the eyesight issues became apparent and Army doctors diagnosed him as suffering from severe retinitis. Eventually, his eyesight was completely taken away by the disease.

Arnie attended the School for the Blind, and there he met and married Kathy, who was also blind. On March 27, 1962, he met the Lord as his personal Savior and was born again by experiencing the miracle of the new birth. Five years later he felt called to the ministry and the family moved to Owatonna to attend Pillsbury.

After graduation Arnie became youth pastor at Grace Baptist Church in Owatonna for a year and a half and took classes at Central Seminary. God gave the Fredricks three lovely daughters, Ranea, Dyann, and Lynda.

Arnie became an evangelist and taught at Great Plains Baptist College in Sioux Falls, South Dakota, where he received his doctorate. After hearing the message which Dr. Fredricks preached at his father's funeral in 1998, his brother Stan Fredricks offered to put Arnie on the radio. He financed *The Touch of the Master's Hand* radio program which Arnie continued for many years. Dr. Fredricks went to be with the Lord in 2015.

Larry Freed

Student: 1988-1990, 1994-1996

Larry punctuated his stints at Pillsbury by serving an enlistment of active duty in the United States Navy. He ultimately completed his BA in Bible in 2002. During his first years at Pillsbury he lettered as a member of the last football team ever fielded by the college. During the second time on campus he was impressed by the fact that even though enrollment was down the desire of the students to serve Christ was just as evident as before. "The true gauge of a person's sincerity or character is how they respond in times of adversity," he writes.

Freed is now preparing for retirement from the Iowa Department of Corrections in six years (not that he is counting the days or anything). He began his career as a Correctional Officer and was eventually promoted to

Case Manager. The position of Case Manager for the Iowa DOC requires a college degree, so Pillsbury was directly involved with his career advancement opportunities.

Larry says, "For those of you who remember me from either of my stints a Pillsbury, I have been "in prison" for over twenty years now—I guess you could say."

Shirley Freed (See Shirley Proffit)

Dorothy (Allen) Freerksen

Student: 1961-1965

Faculty: 1968-1975

Dorothy married Jim Freerksen after graduation in 1965 and settled in Minneapolis while Jim completed his work at Central Seminary. From there they moved to Rawlins, Wyoming, to start a church. When the opportunity came for Jim to teach Greek at Pillsbury, they returned to Owatonna and stayed for seven years.

Dorothy taught courses in Children's Ministry and headed up the daycare for faculty children.

Freerksen felt a need for more training which took place at Grace Seminary in Winona Lake, Indiana. Dorothy again worked in a daycare and then as a pastor's wife when they accepted the call to be interim at Wawasee Heights Baptist Church. After graduation the Lord led them to Lynchburg, Virginia, and Liberty University.

Dorothy worked in the Children's Ministry at Thomas Road Baptist Church, overseeing primary teachers and writing missions curriculum. In 1997 Jim was asked to be part-time pastor at Berean Baptist Church in Lynchburg. They ministered there for seven years, seeing the mortgage paid off and a full-time pastor called, and then continued in that church for another twelve years. During that time Dorothy managed the church library.

The Freerksen's daughter, Amy, her husband David Boardwine, and her family are active in a church in Lynchburg. Dorothy and Jim's son Brian, along with his wife Nancy and family, serves as youth pastor in another Baptist church in town. Since Jim's retirement in 2014 the Freerksens have visited Hawaii, Alaska and the Caribbean.

James Freerksen

Student: 1958-1962

Faculty: 1968-1975

Jim enrolled at Central Baptist Theological Seminary of Minneapolis after graduation and completed his MDiv degree. He married Dorothy Allen in Laurel, Montana, during the summer of 1965 and they lived in Minneapolis while he finished at Central. From there they moved to Rawlins, Wyoming, to start a church. On the advice of several individuals who recognized his giftedness in teaching, he accepted a position as professor of Greek and Bible at Pillsbury in 1968. During the next seven years he taught numerous classes and earned his ThM from Central.

Feeling the need for additional education, the Freerksens moved to Winona Lake, Indiana, so Jim could work on his ThD at Grace Seminary. They began to attend Wawasee Heights Baptist Church in Syracuse, Indiana, and soon the church asked him to serve as Interim Pastor. He was ordained by that church.

After finishing his residential doctoral work, the family moved to Lynchburg, Virginia. Jim taught New Testament and Greek at Liberty University while writing his doctoral dissertation, *The Biblical Role of Women with an Exegesis of I Corinthians 11:2-16*. After several years teaching undergraduates, Jim was asked to join the seminary faculty and remained in that position for twenty-three years. During that time Dorothy and Jim made three trips to Holland for Jim to teach in the Greater Europe Mission Seminary. He also served seven years as pastor of Berean Baptist Church in Lynchburg.

Jim has written the commentary on Hebrews for the *Liberty Bible Commentary* as well as notes for Acts, James and New Testament Background for the *Liberty Annotated Study Bible*. Articles include "Shall We, Then, Live by Grace?" for the *Fundamentalist Journal*, and "Acts" and "James" for the *Popular Encyclopedia of Bible Prophecy.* He retired from teaching in 2014.

Bernie Frey

Student: 1957-1961

When Bernie Frey enrolled at Pillsbury in the very first class, his daughter Barb and son Duane were among his fellow classmates. He felt the call of God into the ministry at age 41 and attended Northwestern Bible College for two years before Pillsbury opened. He purchased a home near campus with only one dollar down and worked as a car salesman to support his family and pay his school bills. He was the first grandfather to graduate from Pillsbury.

When Dr. Monroe Parker came in 1958 as the first resident President of the college, Bernie often went to him for advice. Dr. Parker would kneel and pray with him about his financial needs and together they would watch God supply. During his student years, Bernie pastored Baptist churches in Cannon City and Waterville, Minnesota.

After graduation Frey served as pastor of First Baptist Church in White, South Dakota and then Calvary

Baptist Church in Wells, Minnesota. In 1972 he became the Coordinator of the New Testament Association of Independent Baptist Churches. During that time, he traveled extensively, representing the Association and encouraging pastors.

Throughout his life, Bernie was a passionate soulwinner. He took time to tell waitresses, gas station attendants, neighbors, family and friends about the Lord and Savior he loved. On April 17, 1974, at the age of 59, Bernie was called home to heaven from a sudden heart attack.

Over the years, twenty-one members of Bernie's family attended Pillsbury, while four of them taught, worked, coached or served on the Board of Trustees. That included all four of the Frey's children, Barb Frey Sherman, Duane Frey, Marcia Frey Schearer and Deb Frey Boldt. Their daughter Deb taught and worked at the college for twenty-three years.

Deb Frey (See Deb Boldt)

Bob Fuller

Student: 1966-1970

Bob graduated from Pillsbury in 1970 and married Jacque Johnson in June. They settled in Minneapolis while Bob completed his MDiv from Central Seminary. He later earned the ThM from Grace Seminary in Winona Lake, Indiana, and the DMin from Central.

The Fullers moved to Fowler, Colorado, to administer the Christian School there after completing seminary. They have also ministered at Coon Rapids Baptist, Valley Baptist, Berean Baptist of Detroit Lakes and First Baptist New Ulm, all in Minnesota.

The Minnesota Baptist Association called Bob to be its State Missionary, serving the churches of the state through publishing, pulpit supply, consulting, encouragement, annual meetings and pastoral counseling. He has also served on various committees and boards for the Association, including the board of Pillsbury Baptist Bible College. Bob and Jacque spend many hours on the road, serving the churches of the MBA. He retired from that position in 2018.

The Fullers have three children, Rhoda Jane and Matthew Olmstead, Rob and Heidi Fuller, and Rebekka and Justin Nelson, as well as eleven grandchildren.

Christina Fuller (See Tom and Christina Hiduk)

Jacque (Johnson) Fuller

Student: 1964-1969

Faculty: 1995-1996

Jacque Johnson Fuller was very active in music during her years at Pillsbury. As a member of the Madrigal Quire, under the direction of Thelma Cedarholm, she traveled for the college. The Quire also played handbells during those years. She and Bob were married in June of 1970. She graduated from Mankato State that year with a BS in Teaching Music. They moved to Minneapolis to attend Central, spent some time in Fowler, Colorado, as administrator and faculty at a Christian school and then returned to Minnesota to minister in Coon Rapids, Valley Baptist, Detroit Lakes and New Ulm, before Bob became the State Missionary for the Minnesota Baptist Association.

Jacque taught school music for over thirty years in the towns where they lived. She also spent twenty years as a part-time Customer Service Representative for Cashwise Foods. She sang with the Minnesota Valley Chorale for twenty years and is now the librarian at Fourth Baptist Christian School. The Fullers have three children, Rhoda Jane and Matthew Olmstead, Rob and Heidi Fuller and Rebekka and Justin Nelson as well as eleven grandchildren.

Pam Funk (See Franco and Pam Minutillo)

Amy Geiszler (See Amy High)

Lorene Gibbons (See Lorene Lambert)

Shelly Gibby (See Shelly Lutzweiler)

Darlene (Sandusky) Gilbert

Student: 1968-1969

Darlene Gilbert attended Pillsbury for one year. When her husband LeRoy graduated they moved to Minneapolis with their daughter Sheri so he could attend Central Seminary. It was a move back home for Darlene who had attended Fourth Baptist previous to her time in Owatonna. She has now been a member at Fourth Baptist Church for fifty-eight years. She has served in that church faithfully in a great variety of ministry areas.

The Gilberts have been blessed with four children, Sheri, Todd, Timothy, and Sarah as well as ten grandchildren. During the 1998-1999 school year they lived in Owatonna once again while LeRoy headed up maintenance at the college. Since 2012 he has been retired. They are thankful for the many opportunities to serve the Lord together and be a witness and testimony for Him.

Duane A. Gilbert

Student: 1957-1961

The summer after graduation, Duane worked on the construction crew for Clearwaters Hall on campus. Moving to Minneapolis, he attended Central Baptist Theological Seminary where he met and married Barbara Bilsborough in 1965. Duane served two years as associate pastor at Calvary Baptist Church in Watertown, Wisconsin, before returning to Minnesota to work with the youth group at Fourth Baptist Church. In May of 1971 he accepted a job as custodian and purchasing agent for Fourth Baptist and remained in that position for the next forty-one years. The Gilberts have two daughters and four grandchildren.

Duane has served as a Neighborhood Council President. He volunteered for eight years with the Brooklyn Park Police Reserves and served five as a professional Security Officer. Working with the youth group, singing in the choir and serving the Lord at Fourth Baptist Church, Fourth Baptist Christian School, Camp Clearwaters and Central Seminary has been the great blessing in Duane's life. Seeing the results of those ministries in the lives of students has been a great reward for years of service.

LeRoy Gilbert

Student: 1965-1970

Staff: 1998-1999

LeRoy and Darlene Gilbert moved to Minneapolis after his graduation and enrolled at Central Seminary. In 1971 he began a career at Medtronics, Inc., which lasted for the next twenty-six and a half years. During the 1998-1999 school year he returned to Pillsbury as Maintenance Supervisor and operated the Power Plant. Moving back to Minneapolis, LeRoy accepted a position as Maintenance Engineer at the Radisson Hotel and Crowne Plaza. He worked there until retirement in 2012.

Gilbert has been a member of Fourth Baptist Church for fifty-two years. During that time he has served as a deacon, Sunday School Superintendent, usher and on the Security team. He also spent many weeks as a counselor at Camp Clearwaters. His expertise in the field of maintenance has been a great blessing to the church both in North Minneapolis and at its present location in Plymouth.

"Pillsbury was a very wise investment for me," writes LeRoy. "Many of my classmates are still dear friends and are serving the cause of Christ around the world. My training at Pillsbury prepared me for ministry at Fourth Baptist Church, the Christian School and Central Seminary."

W. Edward Glenny

Student: 1968-1972

Faculty: 1975-1982

W. Edward Glenny completed his MDiv and ThM degrees at Central Seminary in 1976 and 1982. He graduated from Dallas Theological Seminary in 1987 with a ThD. His dissertation was on "The Hermeneutics of the Use of the Old Testament in I

Peter." In 2007 he earned a PhD from the University of Minnesota, in Greek. That dissertation was titled "Translation Technique in the Septuagint of Amos."

Dr. Glenny taught New Testament and Bible Exposition at Central from 1984-1999. He has also served as an adjunct or visiting professor at Maranatha, Northland, the University of Minnesota, Bethlehem College and Seminary, and Bethel Seminary. Since 1999 he has been a Professor of New Testament and Greek at the University of Northwestern-St. Paul.

Ed has published more than thirty-five scholarly reviews, articles and essays in the *Journal of the Evangelical Theological Society, Review of Biblical Literature, Religious Studies Review, The Journal of Hebrew Scripture, Bulletin for Biblical Research, Bibliotheca Sacra and Grace Theological Journal* among others. He has written the commentaries *Micah, Amos and Hosea* for the *Septuagint Commentary Series.* Books which are contracted for the future include *Ruth,* and *The Twelve (3 volumes)* in the *Septuagint Commentary Series, I Peter* in the *Evangelical Exegetical Commentary Series,* and *Amos* in the *Baylor Handbook in the LXX Series.*

Dr. Glenny holds membership in the Evangelical Theological Society, the Institute for Biblical Research, the International Organization for Septuagint and Cognate Studies and the Society of Biblical Literature. He speaks often in churches, colleges and at retreats and conferences. He has served as interim pastor on fourteen separate occasions, has participated in short-term missionary work in France, Romania and India and organized and led study groups to Israel, Turkey and Great Britain.

Jackie (Anderson) Glenny

Student: 1968 – 1971

Faculty: 1975-1982

Jackie Glenny continued her education at the Goethe Institute in Germany, the Institute of Holy Land Studies in Jerusalem, Israel, and Dallas Theological Seminary in Dallas, Texas. She earned her Master of Business Communication from the University of St. Thomas in St. Paul, Minnesota, in 1992 and her Doctorate in Educational Leadership from the University of St. Thomas in 1998.

Dr. Glenny taught at Fourth Baptist Christian School for twelve years as well as the Minneapolis Business College. Since 1993 she has been Professor of Communication at the University of Northwestern-St. Paul. She is a member of several professional organizations including the National Communication Association, the National Religious Communication Association, the Communication and Theatre Association of Minnesota, the Twin Cities Forensic League, the Minnesota Speech Coaches' Association, the Minnesota Education Theater Association and the Business Communication Network.

Jackie has made scholarly presentations at numerous conferences. She is the author of *"The Gainey Experience: The Life and Leadership of Daniel C. Gainey,* and *"C. S. Lewis's Cambridge: A Walking Tour.* One of the highlights of her sabbaticals has been the opportunity to conduct lecture/guided tours in Cambridge, UK, for Christian Heritage at the Round Church.

The Glennys are members of Bethlehem Baptist Church in Minneapolis. Jackie speaks frequently to women's groups, luncheons, conferences and retreats on topics related to C. S. Lewis or "Lady Wisdom" from Proverbs. Jackie and Ed also present sessions for couples retreats on "Unity in Marriage."

Rick and Deb Gnemi

Student: 1971

Faculty: 1978-1983

Rick came to Pillsbury from Hobart, Indiana because his uncle, Russell Dell, was the Academic Dean. He stayed for one year and then transferred to Mankato State to work on a business administration degree. Deb was from Owatonna and they married in 1975. The Gnemis purchased a beautiful home on Cedar Street and have been refurbishing the Victorian home since that time. Rick's appraisal business is in the basement.

In 1978, Rick started working for Pillsbury in the business area, helping with finances and budgets. His title was Financial Consultant, and he helped the college get back in the black during those years. In that position he helped in the purchase of Cedar Court where many of the single faculty lived. He supervised the complete remodeling of the President's house, the guest house on campus and the reception room in Old Main.

When KRPC was on the air, Rick recorded a weekly financial radio show with Randy Miller. He also spoke to future pastors in class about their personal and church finances. Randy says, "Rick was basically a wise Dave Ramsey type before there was a Dave Ramsey."

Rick and Deb have stayed involved in the Owatonna community through the years. As an appraiser he knows most of the people in town and has their respect. He is active as a deacon at Cornerstone Evangelical Free Church. The Gnemis still continue to purchase older homes and restore them to their former beauty. And according to Randy Miller, "he still edges his lawn with a pair of carpet shears."

Karen (Budke) Goblirsch

Student: 1964-1965

Karen worked for Control Data Corporation in Minneapolis after Pillsbury and met her husband John who came to know the Lord through her testimony and the ministry of Fourth Baptist Church. They married in 1969 and have four children, Steve, Chris, Tom and Kathy Jo. She spent twenty-five years with Control Data and then another eighteen with the Schwan's Food Company in Marshall, Minnesota, before retiring.

The Goblirsch's are members of the First Baptist Church of Marshall. Karen continues to sing, for which she gives a great thank-you to Mrs. Kettenring and the voice lessons at Pillsbury. She teaches a ladies Sunday School class and works in Junior church and the K4 program.

Karen's many years in the workplace provided numerous opportunities to witness, a privilege which leaves her eternally grateful.

Deb Goff (See Deb Hudson)

Randy Golightly

Student: 1980-1985

Rodney enrolled at Central Seminary after Pillsbury and then became the High School Supervisor at Temple Christian Academy in Fremont, Ohio. He married Jacqueline Barnes in August of 1988 and attended Detroit Baptist Seminary in 1988-1989. God has given the Golightlys two children, Katharine and Michael.

Rodney has served as Assistant Pastor at Plymouth Baptist Church in Plymouth, Michigan, and Colonial Baptist Church of Galesburg, Illinois. From 1993-2002 he pastored the Oak Street Baptist Church of Durand, Michigan. Since 2003 he has been the Associate Pastor of Faith Baptist Church, St. Paul, Minnesota, and Administrator of Faith Baptist Christian Schools.

While in Michigan he served as a Board Member of the Independent Fundamental Baptist Association of Michigan. He currently serves as a Board Member of the Minnesota Baptist Association.

"I am thankful beyond measure to have graduated from Pillsbury Baptist Bible College, and I cherish my education, training, and friendships cultivated there," writes Rodney. "I am blessed with a godly, loving wife, and we share a joyful, loving home. Currently I serve with my dear friend since high school, Dr. Julian Suarez, as his associate."

Joyce (Odens) Goodwin

Student: 1963-1967

Faculty: 1967-1969, 1971-1978

Joyce Odens taught music at Pillsbury after graduation and then moved to Greenville, South Carolina, to earn her Master in Music degree from Bob Jones University in 1971, before returning to join the music faculty at Pillsbury. In 1978 she accepted an invitation from Evangelist Jerry Sivnksty and his family to travel with them and provide music for their evangelistic meetings. During those travels she met David Goodwin, and they were married in 1979. David is a piano technician and plays bass trombone in brass bands. They have served the Lord together musically in the churches where he has served as minister of music or pastor.

Joyce began teaching private piano during her senior year at Pillsbury and continues to have a private studio. At least ten of her former students are now piano teachers, and many are serving in local churches as pianists and organists. From 2005-2017 Joyce worked as accompanist for the choirs in grades 5-12 in the Owensboro Public Schools in Owensboro, Kentucky.

For eight years Joyce and a friend, Joy Malone, whom God brought into her life, served the Lord together as duo-pianists or pianist/organist in churches, concerts, and community productions until the Lord took Joy home in 2017. To have such an outstanding partner at the keyboards was a special blessing.

Joyce continues to focus on private students in her studio while also serving two churches as organist/pianist, as well as accompanying community and college performances. She has published three books of piano arrangements.

Lynda Grantham (See Lynda England)

Charlie Green

Student: 1986-1996

Charlie Green was the oldest student ever to attend Pillsbury. He enrolled when he was 68, after retiring from the Trane Company in LaCrosse, Wisconsin. Charlie had also served in the United States Navy. He decided to minor in Greek (which is difficult even for a younger learner) along with his Bible major and stuck with that plan for ten years until graduation. Randy Miller set up a special computer for him in the library conference room where the letters were almost three inches tall to help him compensate for his declining eyesight. While a student, Charlie listened to AWANA verses at Grace Baptist of Owatonna. Charlie desired to be used of God, perhaps in ministering and preaching to senior citizens, but his declining health never allowed that.

Charlie also developed Bell's Palsy and one side of his face drooped. He had his own apartment, but finally realized that he couldn't care for himself, so he moved into the West Side Board and Lodge assisted living facility in Owatonna. Randy gave him a cassette player and a special radio which picked up broadcasts for those with visual impairments. He also ordered Christian Talking Books from the Library of Congress Services for the Blind. Charlie died at age 80 on the day before Thanksgiving in 1998.

Robert Griffin

Student: 1966-1968

Faculty: 1996-2000

Robert completed his BA degree at Maranatha Baptist University and has continued his education throughout the years. He holds a BA and MS from University of Wisconsin at Stevens Point, a DMin from Trinity Theological Seminary in Newburgh, Indiana, and the EdD from Calvary College and Graduate School in Dallas, Texas.

Bob married Teresa Bohren in 1970 and they have two sons and a daughter who are all in full-time Christian service. He was ordained in 1973 and certified in counseling in 1977. Griffin has served three churches in pastorates, and Bob has also volunteered as a Chaplain in the U.S. Navy. While in Wisconsin he edited the Badger Baptist Magazine. From 1996 to 2000 Bob taught Bible and Pastoral courses at Pillsbury, commuting from Wyoming. Since 1988 he has served as a Missionary/Church Planter in Wyoming, currently pastoring the Sovereign Grace Reformed Baptist Church of Casper.

Christian Education has been a focal point of Bob's ministry throughout the years. He has traveled to every state and all but one Canadian province as well as to twenty-five other countries as a lecturer on Christian education and has published more than thirty books, workbooks and pamphlets on the subject. He loves to participate as a re-enactor of Civil War scenes playing the part of the 3rd US Volunteer Infantry and 5th Texas Regiment of Hood's Brigade. He proudly boasts of smuggling Bibles into the USSR and Eastern Europe. Archeological tours have included digs in Israel, Egypt, Jordan, Turkey and Greece. Bob and Teresa home-schooled their children from grades 7-12 and now relax on Cruise Voyages. While at Pillsbury, "Dr. Bob" started the Grif-Net, a daily feed of humor and commentary originally sent by email and now shared on Facebook and on the web at grif.net.

Teresa (Bohren) Griffin

Student: 1966-1968

Faculty Wife: 1996-2000

Teresa completed her BA at Maranatha Baptist University in Watertown, Wisconsin. She followed that with an MA in Education from Calvary College and Graduate School in Dallas, Texas, and a Naturopathic Doctorate from Clayton School of Health in Birmingham, Alabama.

Teresa has enjoyed being a pastor's wife, piano teacher and mother. Their son Jeremiah serves with the North American Mission Board as a church planter. Joshua is the founder of "Download Youth Ministries." Lyssa Swolanek is married to a professor at Maranatha Baptist University and runs "Song of My Heart Stampers."

While in Dallas, Teresa wrote curriculum for Accelerated Christian Education and served as a professor in Education at the International Institute. She has been a certified health/nutrition consultant since 1988 and founded the Preventive Health Resources Clinic in Wyoming in 1993. She has spent twenty-five years running a single-doctor alternative health clinic, writing, and lecturing in seminars around the world including China, Hong Kong and Hawaii. She has had hundreds of children's stories published. One of her great joys in life is the privilege of spoiling her grandchildren.

Amanda Grotzke (See Tim and Amanda Miller)

Dave and Cindy (Phillips) Grotzke

Student: Dave – 1970-1974

Student: Cindy – 1972-1974

Dave and Cindy Grotzke married in 1974 and moved to Minneapolis where Dave earned his MDiv from Central. He served as Assistant Pastor and then Senior

Pastor at Bryant Avenue Baptist Church in Minneapolis for fifteen years. In 1990 he accepted the call to become Senior Pastor at First Baptist Church of Brainerd/Baxter. Dave has pastored that church for twenty-eight years. He is also the Administrator of Lake Region Christian School, whose principal is Steve Ogren, another Pillsbury graduate.

Pastor Grotzke and his wife Cindy have been active in teaching, counseling, showing hospitality and participation in the community. They have personally visited many of the missionaries the church supports.

"We are thankful for the basis of Biblical education for ourselves and our children," writes Grotzke. All of the Grotzke children graduated from Pillsbury with the exception of Ben who was a student there in 2008 when it closed. Heather and John Hagen are in business and work with youth in their church. Heather serves as a women's counselor. Nate and Darla Grotzke work in a business and he serves as a deacon. Seth and Crystal Grotzke are missionaries in Spain. Amanda and Tim Miller are in business and serve as youth workers. Tim is also a deacon at First Baptist Church of Baxter.

Seth and Crystal (Barringer) Grotzke

Student: 2002-2006

The Grotzkes have ministered at Lake Region Christian School and Fourth Baptist Christian School on the faculty. Seth served as associate pastor to Dr. Don Odens at Liberty Baptist Church. They worked with Baptist Mid Missions in Peru for a brief time and are now living in Ponferrado, Spain. Their work involves church planting and theological education with Baptist Mid Missions in northwest Spain. They are currently planting a church in Ponferrada while also assisting the Bible institute, Seminario Bíblico Bautista de España, by teaching in various locations around Spain.

Seth and Crystal have one daughter, Tanzen, who "sings, dances, and does all things pertaining to five-year-olds." Seth has published a book on Amazon which he wrote for Tanzen, called *Would Daddy Love Me More?* The Grotzkes value the friendships they made at Pillsbury and thank the Lord that He used their professors to encourage and motivate them to pursue Christ. Looking back on Pillsbury days they thank God for how He used the college in their lives and taught them to trust His faithfulness to His future promises.

Casey Gustafson

Student: 1991-1993

Casey Gustafson and his wife Naomi live in Iowa City, Iowa. They are active in the Faith Baptist Church, pastored by Tim Waldron. God has given the Gustafsons four boys, and Casey is thankful for how "God has blessed my marriage and my career."

Casey is an engineer in a consumer products company in Iowa City. In the church he serves in the area of leading worship along with several other men. "Each time I engage in public speaking, whether in church or at work, I recall being on the Pillsbury Players drama team in 1992," writes Casey.

Eva Jean Hack (See Samuel and Eva Telloyan)

Patricia Hall (See Patricia Potter)

Marnee Hanschen (See Marnee Brandenburg)

Darla Hanson (See Edward and Darla Stricklin)

Diane Harris (See Scott and Diane Moffitt)

Rich and Michelle (Deckert) Harris

Student: Rich – 1984-1988

Student: Michelle – 1985-1989

Rich and Michelle Deckert married soon after graduation and taught abroad for a time before returning to the states. They now teach at Schaeffer Academy, a classical Christian school in Rochester, Minnesota. God has blessed them with four children. Michelle's father, Wayne, long-time Pillsbury professor and coach, has taught all four of the children high school biology which has been a great blessing.

One of the greatest blessings for the Harris' has been their twenty-seven years of marriage as well as their children. Michelle's encounter with metastatic breast cancer has brought the entire family closer together and taught them greater faith and trust in Christ.

Janice "Jan" Hart (See Janice Baker)

Sharon Hartsock (See Dennis and Sharon Fitzgerald)

Chris and Emily (Allen) Haynes

Student: Chris – 2002-2006

Student: Emily – 2001-2005

Chris and Emily moved to Washington state after their marriage and Chris became Music Minister at Galilee

Baptist Church in Kent, Washington. He teaches Bible, Music and History at Cascade Vista Baptist School.

Emily has served in a variety of church ministries and currently teaches first grade at Cascade Vista Baptist School. She also teaches private violin and piano lessons. God has given the Haynes three daughters. One of their great joys is visiting the many interesting sites in Seattle and the surrounding area.

Jim Hazewinkel

Faculty: 1971-1991

Jim and his twin brother Dave started wrestling in 1960 at Anoka High School in Minnesota. He attended St. Cloud State University from 1962-1970, which included years of service in the U. S. Army. The twins wrestled for the all-Army team. At St. Cloud State Jim became a two-time Northern Intercollegiate Conference Champion and a four-time NAIA National Champion. Starting in 1966, Hazewinkel made seven USA teams in a row, competing in the 1968 games in Mexico City and the 1972 games in Munich, Germany. He was a Greco-Roman wrestler.

In 1971 Jim became head wrestling coach at Pillsbury. His teams won two Little College National Titles. On the first day of each semester he would introduce his Physical Education classes with comments like "If you draw significant blood in my class you get an automatic A."

In 1991, Jim moved to Pensacola, Florida, and became head wrestling coach at Pensacola Christian College. He inaugurated the first wrestling team at Pensacola and won four NCCAA National titles and two NCWA National titles. In 2006 he moved to Marion, Alabama, where he taught and coached at Marion Military Institute.

Jim was voted a national coach of the year on six separate occasions. In 1975 he was inducted into the NAIA National Wrestling Hall of Fame. In 1983 he became a member of the St. Cloud State Hall of Fame. 1997 saw him take his place in the Minnesota State Wrestling Hall of Fame. In 2004 he was again inducted into the St. Cloud State Hall of Fame, this time with the team from 1963. The National Wrestling Hall of Fame honored him in 2004 with the Lifetime Service to Wrestling Award, and in 2007 the National Collegiate Wrestling Hall of Fame inducted him. The NSIC Hall of Fame was the seventh such honor accorded to him.

Jim retired from teaching and coaching in 2016 and works with LegalShield in Clanton, Alabama.

Peter and Janet (Sailors) Helland

Student: Peter -- 1974-1976

Student: Janet – 1973-1977

Peter and Janet were married in 1977. He attended Central Seminary and graduated in 1980. He has been serving in the pastorate since that time. They served nearly ten years in South Dakota and five in Illinois. Since 1995 Pete has been on the pastoral staff of Grace Bible Church in the Indianapolis/Greenwood area of Indiana.

God has blessed the Hellands with three wonderful children and eight grandchildren. "We are thankful for the education we received at Pillsbury," they write.

Christopher Herndon

Student: 1989-1992

Chris Herndon moved to Minneapolis after graduation to attend Central Seminary. From there he transferred to Dallas Theological Seminary and completed the work for his ThM in 1998. For the next several years he worked as an electrician and then in 2012 became the facilities manager for Capitol Hill Baptist Church. He considers himself blessed to be redeemed by God, preserved by Him and part of a wonderful church where he can serve.

Chris and his wife Martha have five children, Jasmine, Grace, Donald, Elijah and Shane. He writes of his days at Pillsbury that he "couldn't have enjoyed it more" and that he "loved every minute of it and learned a great deal."

Tom and Christina (Fuller) Hiduk

Student: Tom – 1988-1992

Student: Christina – 1990-1992

As a security guard, Tom had the responsibility of walking the switchboard operator back to the dorm when Old Main closed in the evening. The operator was Christina Fuller and they were married in Sacramento, California in 1992 after Tom graduated. They moved to Lansdale, Pennsylvania where he earned a Master of Arts in Theological Education of Youth from Calvary Seminary. His decision to attend Calvary came from a heart set on youth ministry because of the influence of John Colyer.

After graduation Tom accepted a position as youth pastor in Fruita, Colorado, working with Pillsbury alumnus Roger Cooper. They spent eleven years in that position. "Pastor Cooper taught me how to teach the stories of Scripture. He called it "exposi-story" preaching," writes Tom. They also became close friends with John and Peggy (Cooper) Katsion.

Although they loved Colorado, the Hiduks felt God calling them back to Pennsylvania start a camp that would resemble the camps they had worked in out west. In 2007 they moved to Bradford County, Pennsylvania and went through the tedious legal process of founding

Stoney Point Camp. Located on 150 acres the camp features a Junior Day Camp designed around wildlife education, teen boys and girls camps with overnight wilderness camping and kayaking, and a horsemanship camp. Tom says, "Today as we work through camp ministry I often ask myself, what would John Colyer do? I cherish those Pillsbury days and I cherish more the friends God gave me through them."

Amy (Geiszler) High

Student: 1984-1988

Amy Geiszler married Jon High in 1990 and they settled in Owatonna where Jon was serving as soccer coach and teaching at Pillsbury. From there they moved to Minneapolis and worked at Fourth Baptist Christian School. When Jon accepted a position at Faith Baptist Bible College in Ankeny, Amy became an Executive Assistant at the college, a position she had filled in various businesses. In 2008 they returned to Minnesota as Jon became the Athletic Director and men's basketball coach at North Central University. Amy worked as an Executive Assistant at Crown College for nine years and then accepted a similar position at North Central.

God has given the Highs three children, all of whom have attended and graduated from North Central University, with the youngest, Jared, completing his degree this school year (2018-2019).

Jon High

Student: 1986-1990

Faculty: 1992-1996

Jon High taught in the Physical Education Department, coached soccer, and served as Dean of Men and Athletic Director at Pillsbury. He married Amy Geiszler in 1990. They spent six years working at Fourth Baptist Christian School and six years on the faculty of Faith Baptist Bible College in Ankeny, Iowa.

In 2008 Jon became the Athletic Director and men's basketball coach at North Central University in Minneapolis. While continuing to coach basketball he took on the added responsibility of teaching in the School of Business and overseeing the Sports Management degree program four years ago.

Jon has enjoyed staying connected with former coaches and teammates from his time playing soccer and basketball at Pillsbury. "The stories of our games have become more epic and legendary through the years," he writes, "but the conversation quickly turns to the friendship and ongoing relationships that we have with each other. As a teacher and coach, there is great joy in seeing former students/players who are now married with kids of their own, prospering, building strong families, and serving the Lord."

Rick Hill

Student: 1968-1972

After graduation Rick worked at Bob Bardwell's Ironwood Springs Christian Ranch in Stewartville, Minnesota. He married Barb Bardwell and they moved to New Ulm to help start the New Ulm Christian School along with Pastor Doug McLachlan.

In 1974 Rick was diagnosed with stage three, embryonal cell carcinoma that quickly spread via his lymphatic system throughout his body. After ten hours of surgery at Mayo Clinic he was scheduled for aggressive chemotherapy with little hope of recovery. Pastor John Ballentine recommended a substance called Laetrile which was available in Tijuana, Mexico. The First Baptist Church in New Ulm paid all his expenses to go to Oasis of Hope for the treatments.

Following the successful treatment of his cancer at Oasis of Hope, Rick returned to New Ulm and became interim pastor since the McLachlans had moved to Grand Blanc, Michigan. Feeling the need for seminary training, Rick enrolled at a seminary in Grand Rapids, Michigan, where his former pastor Dr. Nick Weins was the Registrar. While at the seminary he promoted his organic diet, fasting, colonics and multiple nutritional supplements. After seminary he entered the world of

127

sales and marketing which has turned out to be exciting
and rewarding.

Rick has written a book about his experiences with
cancer called *The Cancer Conundrum.*

Kathie Hoehm (See Ron and Kathie Brewer)

Arlis Hoff (See David and Arlis Broome)

Robert W. Holderer

Faculty: 1976-1981

Robert moved from Owatonna to Watertown,
Wisconsin, to become an English professor at
Maranatha Baptist Bible College. In 1986 he entered a
PhD program at Oklahoma State University and served
as a Teaching Associate while earning his PhD in
English Composition and Rhetoric. Beginning in 1990
he became Director of Developmental programs at
Barton County Community College in Great Bend,
Kansas. Since 1993 he has been at Edinboro University
of Pennsylvania where he is Assistant Chair of the
English Department and Director of the University
Writing Center.

Dr. Holderer is the organist and choir director at New
Hope Presbyterian Church in Erie, Pennsylvania. He

served on the Board of Trustees of the Bethesda
Lutheran Services from 2010-2017, and the Board of
Thiel College from 2011-2014. He has presented at
numerous national and regional conferences for the
teaching of writing, most recently in Seattle,
Washington.

Wendy Holm (See Wendy Miller)

Beth Holmes (See Jason and Beth Webster)

Rachael (Keep) Hubbard

Student: 1991-1994

Rachael Keep was involved in many of the dramatic
productions on campus during her time at Pillsbury.
Moving back to the east coast after graduation she
became involved in the Little Theater of Alexandria.
Her directing of Dickens *Christmas Carol* became a

favorite for theater-goers in that area. She has also been involved in various acting roles at the same place.

Mark Hubbard and Rachael were married in 2000. They lived close to the Pentagon, and their lives changed dramatically on September 11, 2001. They witnessed the destruction at the Pentagon first-hand. During the days after the attack they met a band of fathers from New York who were all firemen and had lost their sons who were also firemen. "Meeting those brave men and learning about their sons inspired me to dedicate my career and free time to serving those who serve us," writes Rachael.

Today, Rachael combines her passion with her vocation by serving as Special Events Manager at the USO Metropolitan Washington-Baltimore. At the height of the conflict following 9/11 she visited Walter Reed Memorial Hospital weekly with trained therapy dogs. She has met the Chiefs of Staff, the Secretary of Defense and too many Senators and Congressmen to count, "but the most inspiring people I meet are the service members," says Rachael. "They do what they do because they love it, and they love America. Service members and their families are my heroes."

Interacting with all levels of the military population and their families has become Rachael's way of putting her faith into action. She serves God by serving those who serve our country.

Andrew Hudson

Student: 1982-1985

Faculty: 1996-2008

Upon graduation Andrew went to Central Seminary and completed the MDiv and ThM degrees. God opened the door for him to teach as an adjunct professor at Central and also to teach Greek in Romania. In 1996 the Hudsons returned to Owatonna where Andrew taught for the next twelve years. He chaired the Bible department for ten years and worked with the drama team and the golf team. After leaving Pillsbury in 2008 he taught for a year at Faith Baptist Bible Institute in Albert Lea while completing his PhD in New Testament. Then the family moved to Watertown, Wisconsin, to teach at Maranatha Baptist Seminary. He continues that ministry now and has also enjoyed the opportunity to teach modules in Singapore and Beirut.

Andrew was ordained to the gospel ministry in 2003. Their family, which includes three children (Elizabeth, Jason and Seth) and one daughter-in-law (Rachel) has served the Lord in several local churches over the years. Andrew has also had the opportunity to preach at many churches, camps and conferences. In 2006 he received the Alumni Citation in Christian Higher Education from Pillsbury.

Deb (Goff) Hudson

Student: 1981-1985

Adjunct Faculty: 1996-2008

Deb Goff and Andy Hudson were married between their junior and senior years in college. After graduation they moved to Minneapolis where she taught at Fourth Baptist Christian Day School for eight years while Andy attended Central. In 1993, God graciously sent them their long-awaited first child, Elizabeth. Soon after their second child, Jason, was born they returned to Owatonna. Deb taught a couple of classes as an adjunct, and took several classes at Pillsbury. Their third child, Seth, was born in Owatonna. Deb also taught piano lessons in her home. The children attended Owatonna Christian School for some years and were also home-schooled for a time.

In 2009, God directed the Hudsons to Watertown, Wisconsin, where Andy began teaching at Maranatha Baptist Seminary. Elizabeth graduated from Maranatha Baptist University with a BA in Music Education in 2017, and an MA in Biblical Counseling in 2018. She teaches K-3 music in Juneau, Wisconsin. Jason graduated from MBU in 2018 with a BA in Social Studies, and married Rachel Glaze in June. They live in Lynchburg, Virginia, where Jason is pursuing a master's degree in public administration. Their youngest, Seth, just completed his first year at MBU, and plans to pursue mathematics or engineering.

Deb worked in the MBU Library for four years, managing periodicals and the student workers. She currently is pursuing her Master of Education degree from MBU.

Stephen L. Huebscher

Student: 1990-1992

Stephen Huebscher married a wonderful Christian woman who got saved at the University of Minnesota. God has given them four children in their twenty-one years of marriage. Stephen pastored a church in Ohio for six years.

Stephen worked with former Pillsbury professor Dr. Michael Heiser doing research for Heiser's book *The Unseen Realm.* The book was published in 2015. He taught Hebrew and Latin part-time while working on his PhD in Old Testament. For three years he served as a Hospice Chaplain and then worked as a hospital chaplain resident at Mayo Clinic in Eau Claire, Wisconsin for a year.

In the fall of 2018, Dr. Huebscher was sworn in as a naval officer in the United States Navy as a Chaplain. "This will be my path, God willing, for the foreseeable future," he writes. Listed among his blessings is the fact that he has been able to teach more than one hundred people how to play piano.

Gregory Huffman

President: 2008

Dr. Gregory Huffman was born in Wisconsin and grew up in Rockford, Illinois. Raised in a godly family, he learned to love God and serve Him with all his heart at an early age. He was saved at the age of six and dedicated his life to full-time Christian service a few years later.

Greg met his wife Ruth as a student at Tennessee Temple University in 1967. They married in the summer of 1968. Upon graduation the Huffmans moved to Florida to assume a position as assistant pastor in a thriving ministry. Two years later he relocated to Albany, Georgia, where he started a church. Twelve years passed, and he was called to be senior pastor at a church in Atlanta. During that ministry he worked on his Masters degree in Biblical Counseling which he was awarded in 1985. Bob Jones granted him a DMin in 1991. His dissertation was written on the topic *Pastoral Burnout in Fundamentalism.*

Moving to Macon, Georgia, Dr. Huffman accepted a pastorate and the presidency of the Georgia Association of Christian Schools, a position held for fifteen years. He also served on the board of the American Association of Christian Schools. For four years he pastored a church in Virginia, leading the church in missions and Christian education, as well as camping and outreach ministries. He became a member of the Board of Trustees at Appalachian Bible College and an adjunct professor at Northland Baptist Bible College and Piedmont College.

By God's divine leadership, Dr. and Mrs. Huffman were led to Pillsbury Baptist Bible College where he assumed the presidency of the college in May of 2008. Shortly after this time, the national economic crisis made it obvious that the fall enrollment would be greatly reduced, and the financial status of the college would become dire. The Board of Trustees made the decision to close the college after several other alternatives were explored and proven to be unfruitful

After the announcement was made, the Lord used Dr. and Mrs. Huffman to "pastor" the faculty, staff, and students during the last months of the college, directing them all to focus on "who God is" rather than "why God has so led," in this situation. He compared the situation at Pillsbury to a death in the family. As with a time of death, there likely will be mourning by those whom the closing touches most closely. He reminded everyone that even though the college would close, it would never die, as it continues to live in the service and ministry of the students and faculty.

In the months after the school closed, Dr. and Mrs. Huffman took an extensive trip to six of the Christian colleges where students transferred, endeavoring to encourage and strengthen these students in their journey with the Lord. He currently serves at Brookside Baptist Church in Brookfield, Wisconsin, as pastor for senior care and counseling. Dr. and Mrs. Huffman have three sons, all of whom are serving in vocational ministry, as well as nine grandchildren.

Joe Humrichous

Student: 1965-1969

From Owatonna, Joe moved to Chattanooga to attend Temple Baptist Theological Seminary graduating in 1972 to became pastor of Calvary Baptist Church in Summerville, Georgia. He pastored Independent Baptist Church in Red Bank, Tennessee, from 1976-1981 and Calvary Baptist of Danville, Illinois, from 1981-2004.

In 2004 Joe began a four-year ministry as a conference speaker with the Bible Prayer Fellowship. He returned to pastoral ministry in 2008 and served at First Baptist Church of Covington, Indiana, until 2017. In 2018 he became the President and Executive Director of the Bible Prayer Fellowship.

Joe embraced the grace that brings salvation during a prayer time for soccer practice led by Coach Clarke Poorman in 1965. During Pillsbury years he was called to preach and met his wife of thirty-six years. Dianne Pehl Humrichous died in 2002.

For the last eleven years Joe has been married to his wife Teresa. They live in the country near West Lebanon, Indiana, and have a blended family of five grown children and thirteen grandchildren. Joe has an office in his home church where he makes training videos and writes blogs for the website paradigm1.org. He has written a book about grace for living and grace for leadership called *The Life of the Vine in the Soul of the Church.* It is available from Shepherds Publishing, a company Joe and fellow pastors started in order to publish their own books and facilitate authors of like-mind.

Kathy Hunt (See Kathy Winters)

Marlene Hunt

Student: 1963-1967

Marlene Hunt rejoices that during her years at Pillsbury and because of the faculty who invested in her life, the convictions of her parents became her own. After graduation she completed a degree at Mankato State University.

Accepting a position in elementary education at a Christian school in Cincinnati, she taught for two years and then for one year in Belvidere, Illinois. After that she worked with Heritage Hall Christian School in Muncie, Indiana for thirty years. She has taught kindergarten, first, second, third and fifth grades and served as elementary supervisor for a time. While in

Muncie she completed work for a Master of Arts in Education with a reading endorsement.

Although she loved teaching, Marlene decided to accept a job in the clerical field. "I know what it is like to work temporary jobs, be down-sized, receive a cancer diagnosis and see it all as part of God's sovereign plan," she writes. Eventually God brought her back to Heritage Hall to work in the office. She has always served in her local church, particularly teaching Sunday School. At the present time she teaches grades one through three.

"I am still learning to trust and lean on Him," says Marlene. "We have such a great God. I love studying His names and attributes."

John Jarvis

Student: 1973-1977

John Jarvis applied to Pillsbury and was not accepted as a student because of his worldly habits. He determined at that time that he would never attend the school. Instead, he enlisted in the United States Air Force and was sent to Vietnam. It was during his time in the Air Force that God worked in his heart. When another opportunity to enroll at Pillsbury became available, John did attend and graduate.

Following graduation John moved to Greenville, South Carolina, and worked for the United States Post Office as a mail carrier, retiring in 2005. He then went back to school to obtain a Mortuary Science degree. He works as a licensed Funeral Director and Embalmer. John is active in Faith Baptist Church of Taylors, South Carolina. He writes, "I am so thankful for what I learned and for the teachers and friends I made."

Sarah Jimenez (See Jeremy and Sarah Stephens)

Brenda Johnson

Student: 1992-1997

Faculty: 2004-2008

Brenda was on the faculty when the college closed in 2008. Since that time, she has worked with four different ministries. She taught at Prior Lake Baptist Academy from 2009-2013. While there she helped them move from an ACE curriculum to a traditional, teacher-based approach. In 2012 she had the privilege of serving for a brief time at the Amazon Valley Academy in Brazil as part of the Network of International Christian Schools. She continued working for NICS as a teacher and curriculum developer for their online school, NorthStar Academy.

Moving to Michigan in 2013, Brenda now teaches at Lake Orion Baptist School. She teaches morning kindergarten and some junior high and high school classes. She loves the church and looks forward each day to working with fabulous students.

Brenda rejoices in the opportunity to be part of various missions trips and Bible studies which have allowed her to reach out with the gospel and grow in her personal walk with Christ. She speaks and shares musically at various women's conferences. Thankful for the time at Pillsbury, she appreciates the way God used those college experiences to prepare her for future ministry in speech, music and education.

Dan and Becky (Rogers) Johnson

Students: Dan – 2000-2004

Student: Becky – 2000-2005

Dan Johnson sang and traveled with various music groups during his time in college. He married Becky Rogers, and after graduation they moved to Twin Falls, Idaho. Dan taught and coached at a Christian school and then transitioned into the youth pastorate. Becky also coached and directed plays while spending most of her time at home with first a daughter and then three boys.

In 2013 the Lord led the Johnsons back to Owatonna where Dan became an Associate Pastor at Grace Baptist Church. Then in 2017 an opportunity came to serve at Central Seminary while Dan finished work on his MDiv. Dan's position was Director of Recruitment and Retention. He participates in the music ministry of Fourth Baptist Church, and sings in the select choir Deo Cantamus of Minnesota. In the fall of 2018 Dan was called to be the Music and Administrative Pastor at Fourth Baptist Church of Plymouth, Minnesota.

Dell and Erma Johnson

Faculty: 1970-1987

Dell Johnson taught Bible at Pillsbury for seventeen years. Moving from Owatonna to Denver, Colorado, in 1987 he became Associate Pastor of Beth Eden Baptist Church of Wheatridge and Administrator of Beth Eden Baptist School.

In 1990 the Johnsons moved to Pensacola, Florida. Dell became Professor of Bible and Department Chair at Pensacola Christian College. He was the founding Dean of Pensacola Theological Seminary and taught in the seminary from 1997-2003.

In 2003 Dr. Johnson became the Ministry Relations Representative at Accelerated Christian Education. He served as Presenter at Christian Education Conventions and speaker at Regional and International Student Conventions, traveling to thirty-four countries. Presently he serves as Academic Dean of Accelerated College of the Bible International in Hendersonville, Tennessee, a position he has held since 2015. Dell and Greg Mutsch have enjoyed working together for many decades, first at Pillsbury, then Colorado, Florida, and finally at ACE.

The Johnsons have three children and fifteen grandchildren.

Ed Johnson

Board of Trustees: 1983-1990

Ed Johnson was the pastor of First Baptist Church of Rosemount, Minnesota. His daughter and son-in-law, Lorri and Paul Ague, as well as his son Rick, served on the faculty and administration of Pillsbury. He received his education from Tennessee Temple University and Temple Baptist Theological Seminary in Chattanooga, Tennessee.

Dr. Johnson spent thirty-five years at First Baptist before retiring as Pastor Emeritus in 2002. He founded the First Baptist Church Christian School in 1971. Johnson served as President and then Executive Director of the Minnesota Association of Christian Schools. He also served on the Board of Directors of the American Association of Christian Schools and the General Council of Baptist Mid-Missions. He was honored with Doctor of Divinity degrees from Hyles-Anderson College and Baptist Christian University.

Dr. Johnson went to be with the Lord after a battle with cancer in 2014.

Jacque Johnson (See Jacque Fuller)

Larry and Sally (Nupson) Johnson

Students: 1971-1975

Board Member: 1990-1996

Larry and Sally Johnson were married the summer before their senior years at Pillsbury at the First Baptist Church of Austin, Minnesota, where they served on extension. God has given them five children, each of whom graduated from Pillsbury or attended until the school closed. They also have seventeen grandchildren.

From Owatonna the Johnsons moved to St. Paul, Minnesota, to teach in Temple Baptist Church and School. Larry also worked with the youth, served as music pastor and coached basketball. During those years he attended Central Seminary, completing his MDiv in 1983. Beginning in 1982 he became assistant pastor of Bryant Avenue Baptist Church in Minneapolis and taught in their Christian school until 1989.

Larry pastored Emmaus Baptist Church of Golden Valley, Minnesota, from 1989 to 1998 when the family returned to Owatonna. There he served as assistant pastor at Grace Baptist Church, and principal of Owatonna Christian School until 2005. At OCS he also coached and taught. Since 2005 he has been the Senior Pastor of Grace Baptist Church in Mankato and Administrator of their Christian school. Sally taught in three different Christian schools and has also homeschooled.

Some of the most memorable moments in pastoral and school ministries for the Johnsons have included preaching expositionally through the Scriptures, counseling, officiating at many weddings and funerals, directing choirs and working many years in camp and Vacation Bible School. It has been a joy to see their family involved in the work of the ministry as well.

Leanne Johnson (See Jerry and Leanne Maart)

Marv and Elaine Johnson

Faculty: Marv – 1981-1986

Faculty: Elaine – 1981-1984; 1991-1995

Pastor Marv Johnson carried on a very effective ministry to college students while serving as a pastor in River Falls, Wisconsin. During his twenty years of ministry many of the students who came to River Falls for an education received Christ and sometimes changed their career goals as a result. Dr. Dell Johnson, who taught at Pillsbury, is a prime example. He went to River Falls to study agriculture and became a Bible scholar and professor instead.

Marv and his wife Elaine moved to Owatonna in 1981. He became Dean of Men and a beloved counselor to the student body. People knew that if they went to Pastor Johnson with a personal struggle, they would receive spiritual help. "If someone was trying to break a bad habit he would work with them, allow them to remain in school, overcome the problem and develop regular accountability to prevent a recurrence," says colleague Randy Miller.

Counseling also took place during a radio program on KRPC. Marv would discuss practical topics from a pastor's perspective and interview guests on the campus network. He served as interim pastor in Lake Benton, Blooming Prairie and Stewartville, Minnesota.

In April of 1986, while preaching regularly at the church in Stewartville, Marv decided to ride his motorcycle to church. While on the back roads from

Owatonna to Stewartville, an anhydrous ammonia truck failed to see him, and he was killed not far from Blooming Prairie.

Elaine continued to serve at Pillsbury for many years as Dean of Women. After leaving Pillsbury she became active in Rachel's Hope, a crisis pregnancy center in Austin, Minnesota. All the Johnson's children attended Pillsbury. Ronn came back to teach there from 1991-1994. Marv is buried in the Forest Hill Cemetery in Owatonna.

John and Michelle (Carroll) Jordan

Student: Michelle – 1980-1981

Student: John – 1979-1981

John and Michelle were married in 1981 and settled in Brooklyn Park, Minnesota. He became the first Internet Sales Manager for the St. Paul Pioneer Press. Along with two others, he invented online tools for law enforcement which are now used by several hundred police departments. In 2002 he ran for the Minnesota House of Representatives and won.

Beginning in 2007, John became Director for two different online business supply companies. Both started from scratch and were honored in the Inc. Magazine's Top 500 Fastest Growing Companies. He ran for a seat on the Brooklyn Park City Council in 2012 and served for a year before the family moved to Elk River. Michelle works for a regional insurance company as office coordinator, handling the daily operations of their Minneapolis office.

The Jordan's have been married thirty-seven years. They have two children, Erik Jordan and Allyson Mancuso, and one grandchild. They love to travel and have cruised to Alaska and New England/Canada.

"My life wasn't together," says John of his Pillsbury years. "I didn't know what to do or where I was going. Yet we both look back at our short time as key to what we are today."

Karolyn Grace Jorgensen (See Karolyn Grace Boston)

Joseph A. "Jay" Kalasnik

Student: 1979-1982

Jay served as an announcer working with Randy Miller at KPRC while a student at Pillsbury. Following graduation, he taught at Waterbury Christian Academy in Waterford, Connecticut before enrolling at Calvary

146

Baptist Seminary. From 1984-1991 he managed a retail store in Harleysville, Pennsylvania.

In 1992 Jay decided to enter law school and enrolled at SUNY Buffalo, completing his JD Degree in 1995. Since that time, he has worked as a general practice attorney in Hanover/York, Pennsylvania. He has been a solo practitioner since 2011.

Dr. Kalasnik serves as a deacon at Cross Keys Fellowship Church in New Oxford. He has been President of a Pro-Life Pregnancy Center, and a Sunday School teacher at the church. He serves his community by providing a source for local high school sports pictures called "Attorney Jay Sports Pics."

John and Peggy (Cooper) Katsion

Student: John – 1988-1992

Student: Peggy – 1990-1993

Faculty: 1992-1997

John's obvious talent in drama obtained a teaching job for him at Pillsbury while he worked on his masters degree at Minnesota State University, Mankato. From 1992-1997 he taught in the Communications

Department, directed plays and hosted Night Light along with Chad Wagner and the Pillsbury Players. From Mankato he went on to earn a PhD in Communication from Regent University in Virginia Beach, VA.

After Pillsbury, John taught at Hannibal-LaGrange University in Hannibal, Missouri, for seven years. There he traveled with a drama team, using some of the Pillsbury Players material, familiar skits like "Importunate Friend" and "Christianstein." Hired by the drama and communications department at Multnomah University, the Katsion family spent four years in Portland, Oregon, before returning to Missouri. At Multnomah John worked with the speech and debate team, investing in future workers and laborers for God's Kingdom. Since then John has served as Associate Professor of Communication Studies at Northwest Missouri State University in Maryville. He teaches communication classes and finds ways to spread the gospel and the grace of God in a secular college setting.

Although thrilled to be an educator on the university level, John has always manifested a heart for the upper elementary grades as well. He speaks often at summer camps, including Trout Creek Bible Camp in Oregon and Hidden Acres Camp and East Iowa Bible Camp in Iowa. To capture and hold the attention of fourth through sixth graders, he has developed what he likes to call "Exposi-Story" preaching. Combining a love for history, speech, the Bible, and storytelling, the sermons share what he finds in the Scripture, while filling in the details. Every episode ends with a cliff-hanger, and "the more disappointed the kids sound, the better I feel about the story," says John. He finds it amazing how

250-300 junior-aged kids can be captivated and moved by merely telling a remarkable story—which the Bible has in bucket-loads.

Peggy and John have both been active in various churches in the places where they have lived. At Laura Street Baptist they participate in youth ministry and lead a young marrieds class. God has given them three sons, Jacob, Lincoln and Elijah. John has recently started a podcast called *Baldhead Bible* available at https://baldheadbible.simplecast.fm/.

Rachael Keep (See Rachael Hubbard)

Joel Kettenring

Faculty: 1958-1967

Joel Kettenring earned a BA from Bryan College in Dayton, Tennessee, and the MDiv from Grace Theological Seminary in Winona Lake, Indiana. The Kettenrings came to Pillsbury in 1958 to teach Bible and Missions. During their time in Owatonna, Joel completed work for his ThM from Central, graduating in 1965.

After Pillsbury, Joel served the Lord in several various positions. Places of ministry included Grace Baptist Church of Boyceville, Wisconsin, Faith Baptist Church

in St. Paul, Minnesota, and First Baptist Church of
Wellington, Ohio. They also spent time in Jamaica
where he worked at Hillview Baptist Church and taught
at Fairview Baptist Bible College in Montego Bay. In
Cleveland, Ohio, he worked for Baptist Mid-Missions,
Baptists for Israel and Remnant Ministries (formerly
the Cleveland Hebrew Mission).

Joel enjoyed preaching and teaching, reading, and
spending time with family and friends. After retirement
the Kettenrings moved to Columbia, North Carolina,
for seven years and then to Chattanooga, Tennessee, to
be near family. Their children include Ken and Cristy
Kettenring of Beavercreek, Ohio, Keith and Rhonda
Kettenring of Ooltewah, Tennessee, Pete and Kristine
Winkler of Ooltewah, and Keven and Stephanie
Kettenring of Ringgold, Georgia. Joel passed away
peacefully from his home in Chattanooga in 2014.

Pauline Kettenring

Student: 1958-1965

Faculty: 1958-1967

Dr. Monroe Parker spoke as evangelist at a Wisconsin
Tent Rally where Pauline was the soloist and her
husband Joel was the song leader. He was seeking
Pillsbury teaching staff for the fall of 1958 and asked if
they would be available. The Kettenrings had just
accepted a call to Grace Baptist in Eau Claire,
Wisconsin, but agreed to travel to Owatonna twice a

week to teach. They soon felt God wanted them on campus full-time and moved to Owatonna in December.

Pauline (Polly) served as a vocal instructor while finishing her BA degree. She says, "for nine wonderful years we were exposed to some of the most dedicated and talented friends in the faculty and student body. We were so enriched, as were our four children, Ken, Keith, Kristine and Kevin."

After leaving Pillsbury the Kettenrings served God faithfully in various pastorates, as well as becoming missionaries to Jamaica and teaching at Fairview Baptist Bible College in Montego Bay. Joel and Pauline also worked for Baptist Mid-Missions as well as Jewish Missions in Cleveland, Ohio. Joel entered glory in 2014. They were married for sixty-six years.

Dorothy (Farrington) Kettlewell

Student: 1963-1967

Dorothy Farrington had known of Pillsbury even before it became a Bible College. Her father pastored in Blooming Prairie and she took piano lessons from Stanley Hahn at the Pillsbury Academy. When she enrolled as a student in 1963 she became class secretary and began working closely with the class treasurer, a young man named Bill Kettlewell.

Dorothy and Bill were married at Woodcrest Baptist Church in 1967 and moved to California where she became secretary to Dr. Archer Weniger. Bill enrolled

at the San Francisco Baptist Seminary and completed
his degree program in 1970. They immediately began
deputation for service in Brazil with Baptist Mid-
Missions, arriving on the field in 1972. The Kettlewells
have served in Brazil from 1972 until 2017.

God has given Dorothy and Bill three children,
Stephanie, Amy and Timothy. "We thank you, Lord,
for allowing us to be a small part of that family of
'Pillsbury Sons and Daughters'," writes Dorothy.
"Wow!"

William "Bill" Kettlewell

Student: 1963-1967

Wrestling Coach: 1965-1967

Bill and Dorothy moved to California after their
wedding where Bill attended San Francisco Baptist
Seminary. They were accepted by Baptist Mid-
Missions for service in Brazil after his graduation from
seminary and arrived on the field in 1972 to begin
language study in Fortaleza.

From 1974-1976 he taught Greek and Bible Doctrine at
the Cariri Baptist Bible College in Juazeiro do Norte.
Beginning in 1977 the Kettlewells were involved in
planting churches in three cities, Campos Sales, Aiuaba
and Sao Domingos. While on furlough in 1976 Bill had
begun aviation training and the use of a 1958 Piper Tri-
Pacer reduced three-hour drives to twenty minute
flights.

In July of 1991 the family moved to Petrolina, Pernambuco to plant another church which was turned over to Brazilian leadership in 1996. From there the Lord opened a door in Aracati where a very fruitful ministry began. Another church plant grew, and three couples went off to Bible college and assumed pastoral ministries in other places. Seeing the need for additional training beyond what the Bible colleges were doing, Bill and others began using "Bible Training Centers for Pastors and Church Leaders." More than one hundred and fifty students have now completed that program across Brazil, as well as in Mozambique and Portugal. A Music Seminar ministry has provided quality Christian music training to more than 250 participants as well.

The Kettlewells left Brazil in 2017 and serve the Lord in Centralia, Washington. Bill says, "Pillsbury Baptist Bible College was a huge stepping stone to take us on such a wonderful life. We too 'stand in awe of the work which Thou hast wrought'."

Curtis Kingsland

Student: 1976-1981

Curtis worked for several years after graduation before enlisting in the United States Army in 1985. From the Army he moved to the Air Force, serving there from 1992-2008. He has been a Department of Defense employee from 1992 up to the present time, soon to be retired.

In the various places where they lived and raised their family, Curtis has served in churches as a bus captain, youth leader, pastor, and soulwinner. His greatest blessing has been in raising their children in a godly family.

Donn and Shirley Kittle

Student: 1957-1960

Board Member and Area Representative: Various years

Donn and Shirley were in Pillsbury's first student body of about ninety members when the school opened in the fall of 1957. They were newly married when they heard about the new college, so they pulled their trailer home from Maxwell, Nebraska, to Owatonna and enrolled. Marvin Jones, a friend in Nebraska, had told them about Pillsbury. They were without much money to live, much less go to college. But God provided all their needs and enabled them to graduate in three years without debt and go on to Central.

During their time at Central, Donn served as youth pastor under Dr. Ernest Pickering and then accepted the call to First Baptist Church of Little Falls, Minnesota. After ten years there, the Kittles moved to Denver to minister at Ridgeview Baptist of Wheatridge, for fifteen years. A move back to Minnesota brought them to Owatonna for a fifteen-year ministry at Grace Baptist Church. He also served as administrator of Owatonna Christian School. During that time the church underwent a major renovation. "It was a joy to conclude forty-seven years of ministry in the church we helped start in 1957," says Pastor Kittle.

Donn retired in 2007. The highlight for him has been in seeing the Gospel ministry provide a life-time of fulfillment, assisting others in their spiritual journey of life. Any effectiveness in seeing people's lives changed by the power of the Gospel he attributes to the foundation Pillsbury gave them. "Even in our sunset years," writes Donn, "we are forever grateful for its influence in our lives through what we learned in class, and how we were shaped by many mentors!"

Kathie Kittle

Student: 1979-1983

Kathie moved back to Denver after graduation and began teaching at Beth Eden Baptist School. She has continued to teach for the past thirty-five years. During that time, she has also served as an assistant principal for twelve years and as a school principal for two years. Kathie has been listed in *Who's Who of American Teachers*.

Kathie thanks God for Pillsbury and her training there. She considers it an honor to be a graduate of the college. Active in her church, she has made two trips to the mission field, one to Mexico and one to Uruguay. She is the author of two children's books, *God's Awesome Power* and *America's Awesome Liberty*. She also wrote a Christmas play called *Candy Cane Lane*.

Alvin William Knutson

Student: 1968-1972

Al Knutson returned to his hometown of Brookings, South Dakota after graduation where he started a church in the living room of their home. He had married his wife Lois in 1966 and they had farmed in the Brookings area before attending college. That church plant became Bible Baptist Church of Brookings. Moving from there he served as pastor in Carlyle, Illinois, and New Castle, Indiana. The last twenty-five years of ministry were spent at Calvary Baptist Church of Manistee, Michigan. Al became known for his charismatic preaching style and his passion for souls. He spoke in revival meetings across the country and visited Mexico and the Philippines as well.

Dr. Knutson was awarded an honorary Doctor of Divinity degree. In addition to serving God and the church, Al was an avid outdoorsman who loved to hunt, fish and garden. He and Lois had two children, Adam and Taffaney. He went to be with the Lord on March 20, 2018.

Anna Lois Kroll

Student: 1976-1982

Library Staff: 1987-1988

Anna Kroll worked at Birdseye in Waseca after graduation to earn money for her MLIS (Masters in Library and Information Science) degree from the University of Wisconsin, Milwaukee. Completing that degree in 1986 she worked a year at Calvary Baptist Seminary in Lansdale, Pennsylvania, returned to work at Pillsbury for a year and then accepted a position at The Master's Seminary. She has worked for The Master's Seminary since that time.

In 1999 Anna traveled to the Ukraine to set up the library for a seminary just outside of Kiev. The next year she traveled to Berlin, Germany, to accomplish the establishment of a library for another seminary. She served a three-year term, first as Secretary, then as Vice-President and President of the Southern California Theological Library Association.

Outside of her career, Anna has been involved in a Christian camping and hiking group. She was Treasurer of the Bible Science Association for several years. They meet once a month and listen to lectures on scientific topics which show evidence for a literal interpretation of Scripture. She serves as a docent for the Santa Clarita Valley Historical Society and has been involved in a variety of volunteer activities at her church.

"Because of God's forgiveness and loving care for me, I can look to the future with hope and joy to see what God will do in my life," writes Anna, "which I still must remind myself when the challenges start to feel scary and overwhelming."

John and Laura (Lyford) Labins

Student: John – 1982-1985

Student: Laura – 1976-1980

Staff: 1985-1987

John and Laura Labins both served on staff at Pillsbury. John pastored Medo Baptist Church in southern Minnesota for four years after graduation. In 1990 he met church planter Harvey Seidel at a mission's conference in southern California. Pastor Seidel had just helped with the reorganization of the Bible Baptist Church of Placerville, California, and was looking for a pastor for the congregation. The Labins visited with the people of Bible Baptist Church and within six weeks had relocated to Placerville where he has served ever since.

Pastor Labins has continued his education with an MRE and an MDiv. He has also completed course work toward his DMin.

Lorene (Gibbons) Lambert

Student: 1985-1990

Lorene moved from Owatonna to Phoenix, Arizona, to work at Tri-City Christian Academy as a secondary English teacher. At Tri-City she met Ed Lambert, the son of one of her fellow teachers and they married in December of 1992. She taught at Tri-City until their first child, a son, Eddie, was born. He was joined in 2002 by a daughter, Cecily. A decision to raise their family in a less urban environment led them to Spokane, Washington, in 2004. Soon after Ed's transfer to Spokane, another daughter, Amelia, joined the family. Together they explored the wonders of the Pacific Northwest, learning to ski and shovel snow. Lorene home-schooled and became involved in teaching others as well through the home-school community. In 2017 she accepted a part-time teaching position at a local classical school.

A life-long desire to write brought Lorene into contact with two publishers, The Well-Trained Mind Press, and Simply Charlotte Mason. She has written four books of narrative history for middle-grade readers including *Who in the World was the Forgotten Explorer: The Story of Amerigo Vespucci, Stories of the Nations: from Count Bismark to Queen Elizabeth II, Ancient Egypt and Her Neighbors*, and *A Castle with Many Rooms*. The book *Stories of the Nations* won a "Best Resource" award from the *Practical Homeschooling* magazine.

Cindy (Refsell) Lamgo

Student: 1980-1984

Cindy Refsell spent the summer after graduation traveling for the college with Will and Becky Rathbun, Ruth Newton and Dan Miller. She then moved to Findlay, Ohio, to teach third grade at Calvary Baptist School. She enjoyed her time with involvement in an active college and career group as well as becoming the soprano soloist for Christmas and Easter cantatas.

After four years, Cindy's mother suggested a move to Denver, Colorado. Mrs. Refsell was serving as church secretary to Dr. Greg Mutsch at Beth Eden Baptist Church and had given Cindy's resume to South Sheridan Baptist School. She was hired to teach English and Home Economics in the junior high school. Two years later she became a graduate assistant at the Lamont School of Music, University of Denver. While working on her MA she participated in several operas and musicals and was awarded a cash prize from the Denver Lyric Opera Guild. She even auditioned for the Metropolitan Opera.

Two weeks before graduation in 1992 she met Byron Lamgo on a blind date. They were married on December 26. As their family began to grow Cindy taught part-time at American Christian Academy and

Westland Christian Academy. By the time all three children were school-age they decided to homeschool. Becoming active in the homeschool enrichment program, Homeschool Etc., she taught music for several years.

During that time she auditioned for the Opera Colorado Chorus and began to perform with that professional company. 'It was a magical time," Cindy writes, "homeschool mom by day, opera singer by night."

The Lamgos became involved with a charter school, the Addenbrooke Classical Academy, as their children started heading off for college. Two years ago, Cindy was promoted to Dean of Philosophy and Curriculum, developing curriculum, student accountability and communication with parents. The school has grown from 62 to 820 in six years.

Lori (Stricklin) Lampron

Student: 1987-1991

After graduation Lori Strickland taught at Tri-City Christian Academy in Tempe, Arizona, from 1991-2002. She married Richard Lampron in 1992. In 2002 she had to step aside from teaching to deal with some health issues for several years. She worked for Staples from 2009-2014 when she stopped working to care for her 95-year-old mother-in-law, who passed away that year. Since then she has been a volunteer in the International Baptist College and Seminary library. The Lamprons attend Tri-City Baptist Church, and Lori works in a ministry called "Joyful Blessings" which ministers to special needs children.

Lori says that two concepts have been the highlights of her life since Pillsbury. She has learned that God loves her for who she is and where she is, rather than for what she can do for Him. That has allowed her to enjoy her relationship with Him. Furthermore, she has learned about the Holy Spirit, that it is her job to submit and His job to work in her. That has resulted in peace and joy.

Darlene Lane (See Darlene Fish)

Irene Larson

Faculty: 1968-1969 and 1990-1991

Irene Larson graduated from Storden High School as valedictorian in 1932 and spent two years at the University of Minnesota before marrying her childhood

163

sweetheart, Emanuel Larson in 1935. She raised three girls and then went back to college and finished a bachelor's and a master's degree in English at Mankato State University. She taught at Pillsbury in the late 1960s before becoming the first full-time English professor at what is now Liberty University in Lynchburg, Virginia. Irene taught at Liberty from 1973-1983.

After retirement, Irene moved back to her hometown of Westbrook, Minnesota. She was a member of the Immanuel Baptist Church in Westbrook and came out of retirement in 1990 to teach another year at Pillsbury. She dearly loved God, enjoyed gardening and music. She played the piano and sang solos in church until she was about 80. Irene passed away August 9, 2015 at 102 years of age.

Penny (Simpson) Latham

Student: 1967, 1990

Penny Simpson came to Pillsbury from Pinole, California, where she got saved at the First Baptist Church in 1961. At Pillsbury, she met Tom Latham and they were married on June 8, 1968. Penny completed her degree from Pillsbury in 1990 and earned a nursing degree in Brazil in 1998.

Penny has served as a missionary in Brazil, alongside her husband, since 1976. They raised their three children on the mission field. Among many of their methods of service on the field, they have collected wedding dresses to help those who had been cohabiting when they came to Christ have a dress when they got married.

Tom Latham

Student: 1965-1969

Tom Latham was raised by his grandparents in Lebanon, Oregon. He served in the Navy during the Vietnam War. On May 6, 1964, he was invited to the Calvary Baptist Church of San Francisco by a fellow sailor on the USS Interceptor. That night he accepted Christ and the next year enrolled at Pillsbury, riding in from California on his motorcycle. He graduated from Central in 1973 and earned his Doctor of Ministry degree from Luther Rice Seminary in 1987.

Tom and his wife Penny applied for missionary work in Brazil in 1973 and arrived on the field October 1, 1976, with their two sons and one daughter. Tom, Jr. was six, Shane was five and Kosette (Kosy) was one. Since that time, they have served in the land of Brazil, starting Baptist churches and turning them over to national pastors. Tom had always liked wrestling, so he started a wrestling ministry as an outreach to the public schools.

The Latham's son, Captain Thomas Latham, is a battalion chaplain in the 107th Airborne, stationed in Italy. Shane and his wife Erin live in Gravatai, Brazil, where they have started several Baptist churches which are now under national leadership. Kosette is married and lives in Alabama.

Tom and Kathy Lawson

Faculty: Tom – 1976-2008

Faculty: Kathy – 1976-1993

Tom and Kathy Lawson arrived on the Pillsbury campus in the fall of 1976 as music faculty. Kathy taught organ and Music Education. Tom directed the band and very soon was invited to become Director of Communications. This job involved overseeing all the audiovisual equipment as well as editing the Bulletin and functioning as the official media spokesman for the college. During the years KRPC was on the air, Tom supervised the radio station. He also had a regular program on air called "Great Moments in Sacred Music." Another aspect of Communications included oversight of the photography lab and eventually the website.

Promotional materials in the form of multi-media slide presentations were the combined effort of Tom Lawson, Ed Cunningham and Randy Miller. Tom would write the script, Ed would provide the photographs and Randy recorded the audio. When the college moved to promotional videos, Tom worked closely with *Sonlight Productions* in the preparation and editing of those films.

When Pillsbury closed Tom was the faculty member with the longest tenure in the history of the college, thirty-two years. The Lawsons moved to Ohio where Tom works for a children's hospital.

Paul and Deanna (Strand) Leslie

Student: Paul – 1967-1971

Student: Deanna – 1969-1971

Paul Leslie was a Chicago boy who moved west after marrying Deanna Strand, who was from Laurel, Montana. He accepted the pastorate of Rocky Mountain Baptist Church in Ennis, Montana in 1973 and remained there until 1987. Paul led the church through a building program, doing much of the work on the church himself along with others in the congregation. He participated in bareback riding in the Ennis rodeo, and was also active in the ministry of Castle Rock Baptist Camp.

In 1988 the Green Corners Baptist Church of Belding, Michigan, called him as pastor, a position he has held up to the present time. In Michigan he has served as

the Belding Police Chaplain since 1991 as well as a
Michigan State Police Chaplain from 2004-2014.

James and Arlene Lewis

Faculty: 1969-1984

James and Arlene Lewis came to Pillsbury in 1969
when James became head of the English Department
and the Education Department. When Barbary Walley
arrived the next year, he was able to concentrate on
Education. James started the observation and student-
aide programs in the college nursery as well as in the
public schools of Owatonna.

Because every student majored in Bible, a full-fledged
Education degree involved a five-year program. By
taking an additional year and doing student teaching,
Education students earned a second bachelor's degree
in Education in addition to their Bible degree. All the
arrangements for student teaching assignments, from
Connecticut to California, fell to the head of the
Department. James also did much of the traveling to
observe student teachers.

James sponsored an annual principals' recruiting conference, a Christian Educator's conference and a yearbook workshop for Christian schools. He and Arlene served as yearbook advisors for twelve years. Lewis also organized the *Orbit* student newspaper. As part of the college wind ensemble, he played the tympani.

After Pillsbury, James and Arlene moved to Oklahoma for twelve years and then to Sioux City, Iowa. He served as administrator and teacher in two different schools during those years. After retiring, he started teaching English as a Second Language to adults in South Sioux City, Nebraska.

The Lewis's have three children, Brenda in Sioux City, Barry and Cheri Lewis in Madison, Wisconsin, and Bethamy and Vince Carrig in Sioux Falls, South Dakota.

Carilee Lind

Student: 1994-1998

During her senior year at Pillsbury, Carilee applied for a position in the payroll and accounting department of Baptist World Mission. She worked for them for seventeen and a half years, providing extensive financial advice and support to missionaries around the world. From there she moved to North Platte, Nebraska, to work with an accounting firm as a CPA. "I didn't learn everything I needed for my future at Pillsbury," says Carilee, "but I did learn to be a continual student of God's Word and of accounting."

In 2001 Carilee earned the Certified Bookkeeper designation from the American Institute of Professional Bookkeepers. She became a Dave Ramsey certified counselor in 2005 and in 2018 earned the Enrolled Agent designation from the Internal Revenue Service.

Dorinda "DJ" Lind (See Dorinda Allen)

Larry Lindow

Student: 1984-1988

Upon graduation from Pillsbury, Larry taught in three various Christian schools over the next seven years. He met Lisa Darling and they were married in 1990. The two of them spent a year as house parents for Baptist Children's Home in Valparaiso, Indiana. In 1995 Larry accepted the call to become Assistant Director at Camp Manitoumi, the camp he had worked at through high school and college. Their next ministry was at Germantown Hills Baptist Church in East Peoria, Illinois, where he became Assistant Pastor for Youth in 2000.

During the ministry in East Peoria, God awakened in Larry an even greater desire to preach. He became pastor at First Baptist Church of Littleton, Illinois, where they spent ten-and-one-half years. In 2016 he became pastor of Cornerstone Baptist Church in Lakeland, Florida.

Larry says his greatest blessing is "seeing individuals who want to hear God's Word proclaimed and then strive to be obedient to it. The highest honor is being allowed to proclaim God's Word on a consistent basis." As a family the Lindows have fostered multiple children, raising them alongside their own, and adopted two who were abandoned by their father. "Watching our children beginning to leave home and have a desire to live for Him is also fantastic," he writes.

Charlotte Lindstrom (See Charlotte Martin)

Kathryn Lindstrom (See Russ and Kathryn Reemtsma)

Larry Livesay

Student: 1965-1968

Staff: 1992-1996

Larry completed his BA degree and a teaching license from Concordia University. He married Crystal

Bookman in 1968 and went on to earn a Master of
Education degree from Central Baptist Theological
Seminary of Minneapolis. He taught elementary school
at Fourth Baptist Christian School and Owatonna
Christian School, sharing his love of reading with his
students. He served on the maintenance staff at the
college for several years.

Larry was known for his love of family, unfailing
kindness, willingness to help anyone in need, sense of
humor, and his incredible ability to whistle. He
enjoyed camping, canoeing, playing board and
computer games, music, bird watching, reading books
to kids, gardening, and eating the food he cooked. He
passed from this life in 2017.

Ellyn (Sorenson) Luther

Student: 1967-1971

Ellyn Sorenson was very active in the music program at
Pillsbury, traveling extensively with the Joybells trio
which included Lynda Moore and Carmen Odens, with
Barb Bardwell as pianist.

Ellyn married Paul Luther, and after the completion of
his seminary training they moved to Champaign,
Illinois, to plant the Faith Baptist Church. In
subsequent churches she has ministered as a Sunday
School teacher, led women's ministries, accompanied
choirs and directed children's choirs. She has operated
a private piano studio all that time.

For eleven years Ellyn taught high school at North Florida Christian School in Tallahassee, Florida. In 2017 she retired as editor of the Institute for Intergovernmental Research. In retirement she enjoys the privilege of teaching piano to eight of her grandchildren. Her greatest blessing in life has been her three children and ten grandchildren.

Tim Luther

Student: 1967-1972

Following graduation from Pillsbury Tim spent several years as a youth pastor in Pennsylvania before enrolling at Tennessee Temple Seminary. He earned a Bachelor of Religious Education and then pastored two churches in Illinois, Faith Bible Church and Colonial Baptist Church.

Returning to Tennessee Temple, Tim finished an MA in School Administration. The rest of his fulltime ministry was spent in Christian School Administration. He is now semi-retired and serves as groundskeeper and all-around handy-man at Coldstream Christian Camp in Adams, Tennessee.

Tim recalls the chapel services in Old Main as being the highlight of his Pillsbury years. His greatest inspiration as a student came from Professor Larry Pettegrew and Professor Raymond Pratt. "They served as constant examples of what a Christian man should be," says Tim. "My Bible education was the foundation for my entire ministry. To this very day I thank Pillsbury for the education I received in Bible."

Jim Lutzweiler

Student: Jim –1964-1968

Jim Lutzweiler married Shelly Gibby, and they moved to Minneapolis where he completed his MDiv in 1972. A Master of Arts in American History was awarded in 1997 with a thesis titled *Santa Anna and Emily D. West at San Jacinto: Who Edits the Editors?*

For several years Jim was involved in real estate sales: brokerage, investments and independent research. Since 1999 he has been Archivist and Rare Book Curator at Southeastern Baptist Theological Seminary in Wake Forest, North Carolina. His duties include the identification and gathering of primary historic materials with emphasis on Southern Baptist and North Carolina Baptist history. He also serves as adjunct professor of American History at Guilford Technical Community College in Jamestown, North Carolina.

Jim has written many papers for professional conferences. They often involve historical records concerning preachers such as Billy Sunday, Billy Graham, and A. C. Dixon. One example would be "Six-Shooter Salvation: The Colorful Career of Clergyman 'Cowboy Crimm'," which was presented at the Texas State Historical Association in Austin, March 3, 2006.

Jim and Shelly have collected hymnals down through the years. The result has become *The James and Shelly Lutzweiler Gospel Hymnal Collection* which was acquired by Liberty University in 2016 and 2018. The total number of hymnals has now grown to 2354.

The Lutzweilers have two sons, Christopher and Nicholas. Jim maintains a personal library of approximately 20,000 volumes which supports his research interests.

Shelly (Gibby) Lutzweiler

Student: 1966-1969

Shelly enrolled at Mankato State after graduation and earned her BS in Speech. She began teaching at Hennepin Technical College in Eden Prairie, Minnesota, and went on to the University of Minnesota to get her MA in Speech Communication. She taught in Minnesota for fifteen years. In 1989 the Lutzweilers moved to North Carolina. Shelly began teaching at Guilford Technical Community College and has been on the faculty there for twenty-nine years. For the past ten years she has served as Department Chair for the Communication and Foreign Language Department.

The Lutzweilers attend a Baptist church in North Carolina, and Shelly works in AWANA. She has also taught Sunday School and Women's Bible Studies. God has given them two sons, a daughter-in-law and "a stupendous granddaughter."

Professionally Shelly has won four excellence-in-teaching awards. She has been a consultant to industry as well as a consultant to others in the college. She is working on two books, one about the school where she works and the other a collection of vignettes about spiritual lessons she has learned. "I will try to get both finished and published when I finally retire, and I haven't decided yet when that will be," she writes.

Laura Lyford (See John and Laura Labins)

Jerry and Leanne (Johnson) Maart

Student: Jerry – 1963-1967

Student: Leanne – 1962-1966

Jerry Maart and Leanne Johnson were married on August 10, 1968. God has blessed them with three children. Jerry has served the Lord in youth pastorates and senior pastorates in Tyler, Minnesota, Laurel, Montana, and Brainerd, Albert Lea, and Stacy, Minnesota. He led a Bible study at the Chisago County Jail for twelve years.

Leanne completed her nurses training after Pillsbury. She has worked at North Memorial Hospital in Robbinsdale, Minnesota, and the Hazeldon Foundation in Center City.

Jerry and Leanne greatly appreciated the impact Pillsbury made on their lives. "We have fond memories of friends, faculty and the stand which the college took," they write.

Don Mackay

Faculty: 1984-1991

Don Mackay worked for the Pennsylvania Game Commission for two years before enrolling at Bob Jones University where he earned degrees in Bible. He married Glenda Baker in 1962. In addition to teaching at Pillsbury Dr. Mackay served as a church pastor and taught at Bible colleges in Florida, California, and Colorado.

After Pillsbury Dr. Mackay pastored in Albert Lea for ten years before retiring in 2001. Following retirement he worked for NAPA and operated a lawn mowing business. He and Glenda became members of Faith Evangelical Free Church in Austin. He enjoyed reading, canoeing, hiking, camping and spending time with family and friends. His greatest joy came from preaching and teaching. Don died in 2015 after a lengthy battle with cancer.

Glenda Mackay

Staff: 1984-1991

Glenda attended Bob Jones University in Greenville, South Carolina and married Donald Mackay on August 11, 1962, in Linesville, Pennsylvania. Don taught at Pillsbury from 1984-1991, and Glenda served as secretary to the Academic Dean, Dr. Charles Baker.

The Mackays served churches and Bible colleges in several states. She was secretary at Grace Community Church in Austin, Minnesota, at the time of her death in 2014. Glenda enjoyed camping, gardening, canoeing, homemaking and teaching children. Their daughter, Becky Mackay Olson lives in Albert Lea, Minnesota, and their son Don and his wife Amanda live in Austin, Minnesota.

Alvin and Evelyn Malmanger

Staff: Alvin – 1975- 1989

Staff: Evelyn – 1975-2005

Alvin Malmanger helped found the Fairmont Photo News in Fairmont, Minnesota, before coming to Pillsbury as the print shop manager in 1975. Much of the Pillsbury equipment was old and difficult to maintain, and he used to joke with Randy Miller about having to work around the equipment rather than working with it. But he was a real craftsman and did a fantastic job.

The print shop did almost all the college printing and mailing in-house. Al printed the *Pillsbury Bulletin*, college catalog, mailings for special events like Harvest Home and College Days, as well as course syllabi and conference notes. He worked closely with Tom Lawson, the Director of Communications. After printing, the huge sheets would be run through the folder and trimmer. At one time the print shop was mailing out over 40,000 copies of the *Bulletin*.

Evelyn ran the mail room. She would prepare all the publications for mailing and also sort and deliver the incoming mail with the help of part-time staff workers. When Al died in 1989 she continued working for the college until retirement in 2005. She completed thirty years of faithful service to the college which helped her celebrate her 80th birthday just before she retired. Evelyn died in 2017.

Curt Malmanger

Faculty: 1973-1984

Curt Malmanger received his BS and MS in Mathematics Education from Bemidji State University. He taught high school math in Menagha, Minnesota, before joining the faculty at Pillsbury in 1973. In addition to teaching math, Curt served as assistant football coach alongside Terry Price. He completed the 36-hour Bible major and received his BS in Bible from Pillsbury.

Dr. Malmanger continued his education and received the PhD in Applied Statistics from the University of Northern Colorado. He began teaching and coaching at Maranatha Baptist University in 1988 until he retired from coaching in 2013.

Kenneth and Vicki (Coats) Mansell

Students: 1979-1981

After eighteen months of deputation, Kenneth and Vicki Mansell left for the field of Japan in October of 1983. They served as missionary trainees under Larry Hagen for two years. In 1985 the Mansells started the Teshio Baptist Bible Church Mission in Hokkaido, Japan. They have continued to serve faithfully in that work up to the present time.

Kenneth earned his Master in Missions for active on-the-field training in 1987. They have mentored more than twenty college students through summer missionary internships as a part of the work of the Teshio Mission. One of the students completed an entire year and another family interned for eighteen months. Both that student and the family remain active in missionary service in Japan.

Charlotte (Lindstrom) Martin

Student: 1974-1979

Charlotte Lindstrom married Jim Martin between her fourth and fifth years of college. They met in choir and his voice teacher, Ron Billingsley, suggested that she accompany his voice lessons. "How could love and marriage not follow?" asks Char. She also greatly appreciated her piano training from Joyce Odens Goodwin.

After graduation they moved to Pennsylvania where Jim attended seminary and Char taught in the Christian elementary school. When Jim became assistant pastor at Calvary Baptist Church in Elkins Park, Pennsylvania, they moved to Philadelphia. Jim became senior pastor of the church when Pastor Mel Hall retired.

All three of the Martin children were home-schooled. As seniors in high school they took History of Civilization from Dave McGuire via recordings, which counted as college credit. All three also attended Pillsbury. "We were thrilled to be back on campus 2001-2008," Charlotte writes concerning those years their children were Pillsbury students. "Many of the faculty and staff became dear friends of ours during those years."

Teaching junior high and senior high girls in Sunday School has been a tremendous joy for Charlotte. She has taught piano and flute for over thirty-five years and loves preparing students for ministry in that way. The Martins are privileged to have in their church first generation immigrants from seventeen different countries. They have come to understand the struggle of a Japanese immigrant to come to terms with "grace" and the Pakistani who finally grasps the concept of "faith." The Lord has allowed them to be the sending church for a ministry to the Arabic-speaking people in Philadelphia.

James Martin

Student: 1975-1979

James Martin married Charlotte Lindstrom on July 28, 1978, and completed his degree from Pillsbury in 1979. Upon graduation they moved to Hatfield, Pennsylvania. James enrolled in Calvary Baptist Theological Seminary, Lansdale and Char began teaching elementary students at Calvary Baptist Christian School.

During his second year in seminary James began commuting to Philadelphia to gain experience in a recent church plant. Upon graduation he was offered the Assistant Pastor position at that church, Calvary Baptist of NE Philadelphia. Pastor Mel Hall retired in 2008, and James became Senior Pastor, a position he still holds today. The church has been able to minister to first generation immigrants from seventeen different countries.

Three children were born to the Martin family, and Char home-schooled each one. All three attended Pillsbury, Melanie graduating in 2004 and James in 2008. Their youngest daughter transferred to Faith Baptist Bible College when Pillsbury closed and completed her degree there in 2009.

James considers meeting his future wife the greatest blessing from his time at Pillsbury. He also appreciated studying music under Ronald Billingsley as well as the Lawsons, Al Lohr and Joyce Odens Goodwin. A highlight of his college experience was traveling with the Pillsbury Bicentennial Quartet the summer of 1976. It was during that summer when James came to the decision to prepare for vocational church ministry.

Susan McClain (See Paul and Susan Van Loh)

Janet (Stevens) McCune

Student: 1974-1978

Janet had the privilege of being a "Seminette" while her husband earned his MDiv at Central Seminary. While he completed his ThM at Grace Seminary in Winona Lake, Indiana, she worked in the Controller's Office. As the pastor's wife at First Baptist Church in Hudson, Michigan, she saw the congregants begin "bringing notebooks to the services because they were amazed at the expository teaching of the word at which their new pastor excelled."

After four years they moved back to Minneapolis and "embarked on a whole new, unexpected path." Janet took a job as an actuary firm to help support the family. "I struggled with arithmetic," she writes, "but at Pillsbury I learned that I was pretty good at comprehending complexity, problem solving, communicating, writing, convincing, organizing and leading." She took the job as secretary and it led to a thirty-year career in this industry.

In 2006 Janet moved to Dallas, Texas, to take a position with Milliman, Incorporated, an international firm of actuaries and consultants, with sixty-two offices around the world and one billion in annual revenue. In 2009 she was elected principal, and in 2011 elected an equity partner. God brought a wonderful partner into her life, and she married John Hunter in September of 2015. Between them they have six children and six grandchildren. They live ten minutes from Stonebriar Church and enjoy the preaching of Dr. Charles Swindoll.

"I always come back to a place of gratitude and humility that God provided Pillsbury, the leaders, the faculty, the students, the convictions and the culture and allowed me to be a student there," says Janet. "Everything I learned at Pillsbury has helped me in every part of my life, and I will always be indebted."

David McGuire

Faculty: 1984-2008

David McGuire taught at Pillsbury from 1984 until the school closed, serving as chairman of the Division of Education and teaching History and Social Studies. The McGuires moved to Greenville, South Carolina, in 2009 to work at Bob Jones University. They had previously been employees there from 1972-1983. Dave helped start the Academic Resource Center in 2009 and worked in that position until 2012. For one year he served as a Customer Service Representative referring customers to potential apartments, and then in 2013 joined Bob Jones Press as a Customer Service Representative.

"Our twenty-five years at Pillsbury and Grace Baptist Church were a wonderful time for us and our children," writes Dave. They have now returned to their previous church, Hampton Park Baptist. Dave sings in the choir during the summer and plays oboe in the church orchestra the rest of the year. They have been privileged to renew connections with friends, colleagues and students from both Bob Jones and Pillsbury as well as other venues of Christian higher education where contacts have been made throughout the years.

Nancy McGuire

Faculty: 1988-2008

Library Director: 1999-2008

David and Nancy McGuire served on the faculty at Pillsbury from 1984 until the school closed in 2008. Dave served as chairman of the Division of Education and taught History and Social Studies. Nancy became the library director in 1999. When Pillsbury closed, she was contacted by the Mack Library Director at Bob Jones University and offered a library position. They moved to Greenville in 2009 and both accepted full-time positions with the University. Six of their seven children continue to live in Owatonna, Waseca and Mankato, so there are many visits back to Minnesota. Their oldest daughter, Cynthia, runs a clinic in Aibai, PNG.

Dave and Nancy count it a great blessing to have taught at Pillsbury among many friends, and teaching students who were eager to learn and serve. Their lives were embedded in the community. Nancy was involved in the public schools as a parent, teaching Junior Great Books, Passport recording, and as a classroom volunteer. She remembers one of her most difficult tasks when the school closed was calling the Director of the Southeast Libraries Cooperating because the college had just gone live with the new Integrated Library System in 2008.

Douglas R. McLachlan

Student: 1966-1967

Board Member: 1972-1974

Doug completed his MDiv at Central in 1970 and became the pastor of First Baptist Church, New Ulm, Minnesota. From there the McLachlans moved to Grand Blanc, Michigan, where he pastored Bethany Baptist Church from 1975-1982. Returning to Minnesota he became pastor of Fourth Baptist Church, serving from 1982-1987.

Dr. McLachlan joined the faculty of Northland Baptist Bible College in 1987 as Chair of the Bible Department. He also managed the Pastoral Graduate Programs. After four years at Northland, Fourth Baptist called him as pastor once again, a position he held until 2007. During those years he served as President of Central Seminary from 1994-2001 and then Chairman of the Board until his retirement.

God has blessed Doug and Marie with three children, Becky Rathbun, Matt McLachlan, and Beth Modaff as well as seven grandchildren and three great-grandchildren. Since retirement he has conducted in itinerant ministry of teaching, preaching in Bible Conferences and writing. Dr. McLachlan has published two books, *Reclaiming Authentic Fundamentalism,* and *Thirsting for Authenticity: Calling the Church to Robust Christianity.*

Lonnie Mead (See Lonnie Williams)

Jim and Terry (Peck) McLeish

Student: Jim – 1968-1970

Student: Terry – 1969-1970

After graduating from Pillsbury in 1970 Jim enrolled at Central. He married Terry Peck in 1971 and completed his MDiv in 1974 and the MRE in 1978. He has done additional work toward the ThM as well.

Jim became a church planter in 1975, moving to Alexandria, Minnesota, and starting a church where he pastored until 2001. There in Alexandria he became involved in political activity with the local Republican party. Baptists for Life of Minnesota invited him to become their director in 2001, and he worked with them in the pro-life cause in the state until 2012.

Since 2007 Jim has been Pastor of Senior Ministries at Fourth Baptist Church. A large group of Golden Agers appreciate his ministry as he organizes activities for them and seeks to encourage them in their spiritual walk. Jim and Terry are so thankful for the way the Lord has led and provided in their lives. They have five children and four grandchildren. Jim writes, "Pillsbury played such a vital, formative role in our future. We are also thankful for all the friends, colleagues and mentors who still remain in our lives because of Pillsbury."

Janet Melchert (See Paul and Janet Sarbaugh)

Thelma Melford (See Thelma Cedarholm)

Jim Mercer

Visiting Professor of Evangelism

Jim Mercer was born in 1913 and was saved in a revival at the Methodist Church of Hosford, Florida, where he grew up. Some local pastors encouraged him to attend Bob Jones College in Cleveland, Tennessee. During college he held numerous evangelistic meetings in which many people were saved. There at the college he also met and married Lois Wilson in 1940.

Jim was known as a man of prayer. His friend and fellow evangelist Billy Graham was once asked in a newspaper interview, "If you had an extreme need, who would you ask to pray for you?" His quick reply was "Jimmy Mercer."

Dr. Mercer spent over fifty-five years in evangelistic crusades all over the United States and Canada. He was a favorite Bible Conference speaker at several Christian colleges and universities as well as Youth for Christ rallies. He served on the board of Bob Jones University and was awarded an honorary Doctor of Divinity degree from his alma mater for excellence in evangelism.

Fall and spring Bible Conferences opened every semester at Pillsbury, and Dr. Mercer was often the evangelist who spoke. He was known for his brief, but pithy sermons. At the first night of one week of meetings he spoke on "Faith" for twelve minutes and sat down. Everyone stayed in their chapel seats, thinking he couldn't possibly be done until he finally stood up and said, "That's it. Faith is faithfulness. Get out of here."

It is a conservative estimate that over the course of fifty-five years of preaching, Dr. Mercer spoke directly to several million people, and God used him to lead thousands to a life-changing personal relationship with Jesus Christ. Jim and Lois spent their last years together in Apalachicola, Florida. He went home to be with the Lord in 1996, holding hands with his daughters and singing "Amazing Grace." Lois died in 2005, and both are buried in the Hosford cemetery within sight of the Methodist church where he got saved.

Drew Meyer

Student: 1984-1988

Staff: 1988-1989

Drew Meyer spent his first year after graduation on staff, helping to set up and run the computer lab for the college. From there he enrolled as a graduate assistant in an MBA program at Mankato State University. Drew accepted a job with the Hendrickson Organ Company in St. Peter, Minnesota, working in the "voicing" section. Voicing is the art and science of manipulating organ pipes to produce the desired tone. The highlight of his three years with Hendrickson was working on a new instrument for St. Joseph Cathedral in Sioux Falls, South Dakota. That instrument contained more than 3000 pipes.

Moving to Sioux Falls, Drew worked for J. F. Nordlie and Company for a time and then for other Sioux Falls companies for the next sixteen years. He became a partner in an organ building and maintenance company, taking care of nearly one hundred and fifty organs in six states until the Great Recession and high gas prices ended that business.

In 2009 Drew moved back to Owatonna to work for HyVee. Not willing to give up the organ business completely, he bought the Allen organ out of Kerux auditorium at Pillsbury. "It waits for the time to give it a new life with more modern electronics," writes Drew. He also serves as organist and caretaker of the organ at First Baptist Church in Owatonna, a gift to that church from none other than Mrs. George Pillsbury.

Kathy (Rosenberg) Michaels

Student: 1974-1978

Kathy married after college, has five children and taught in Christian schools for over twenty years. She considers it a wonderful blessing to be able to teach and mold young lives for Christ.

Grace Midgley (See Virgil and Grace Schuck)

Tim and Nancy (Schadow) Mielke

Student: Tim – 2000-2006

Student: Nancy – 2004-2007

Tim Mielke graduated from Pillsbury in 2006 and then taught photography until the college closed in 2008. During that time he and Nancy started Milky Way Photography. In the fall of 2008 he enrolled at the Academy of Art University to work on his MFA.

Maranatha Baptist University invited Tim to join their faculty in 2009 to teach photography and videography. In order to facilitate his teaching requirements, Tim earned an MA in Multimedia Communications and then went on to complete the MFA in 2017.

"Photography is fundamentally painting with light," says Tim in an article which appeared in *VoyageATL*.

"Using the tools of the camera and computer, I craft light and pixels to create worlds that exalt and reflect the master Designer. My goal is to encourage believers and non-believers to meditate on the ancient truths of Scripture in a personally relevant, contemporary context. My prayer is that my artistic exploration may also help you to know the loving God, the Author of light, in a personal and eternal relationship."

Tim's photography has been exhibited in numerous churches as well as at Concordia University, St. Louis, The VCY American TV program "In Focus," at the Athanatos Festival and the Academy of Art University. He has published an album of photographs called *Dust to Life–The Visual Gospel*. His work is available for viewing online at his website https://www.milkywayphotography.com/dust2life.

Earl and Gloria Miller

Faculty: 1967-1969

Earl accepted Christ as Savior at age 17 while a student at Pineville High School in Wyoming County, West Virginia. Pineville High inducted him into their Hall of

Fame for his excellent baseball career. From there he went to Bob Jones University where he completed the BA in Fine Arts as well as a Bachelor of Divinity degree. His MA was earned from West Virginia College of Graduate Studies.

The Millers moved to Owatonna in 1967 where both Earl and his wife Gloria taught speech and drama courses. Earl is also remembered for his expertise in the fields of Ethics and Logic. When Gloria directed *Macbeth*, he played the title role. Another milestone in those years was the production of *Inherit the Wind*, complete with a live monkey as part of the cast.

Earl began his ministry as a church planter in Ravenswood, West Virginia, and after Pillsbury pastored several other churches as well. He served as a high school teacher for a time and as a college professor at Liberty University. At the time of his retirement he was teaching at Southern West Virginia Community College.

A life-long learner, Earl earned his Doctor of Ministry from Southern Baptist Theological Seminary in Louisville, Kentucky, at age 70. He self-published several works, loved the arts and education, and dedicated himself throughout life to the teaching and preaching of God's Word. He and his wife Gloria celebrated sixty-four years of marriage before he graduated to glory in 2017.

Ernie and Rachel (Zoschke) Miller

Faculty: Ernie -- 2003-2008

Faculty: Rachel – 2000-2008

Ernie attended Maranatha Baptist Bible College for his undergraduate degree and an MA in Biblical Studies. He then continued his education at Central, earning both the MDiv and ThM. He joined the faculty at Pillsbury in 2003, teaching Bible, theology and Greek. He was part of the final faculty when the school closed. Ernie married Rachel Zoschke, who was teaching English at the college when he came. Rachel earned her BA and MA from Bob Jones University and also studied at Oxford University in Oxford, England.

In 2009 Pastor Miller accepted the call to Edmonton Bible Baptist Church in Canada where he served until his death in 2015, after a painful struggle with melanoma. He left behind his young widow and four precious children. Randy Miller wrote at that time that "he was blessed to see what Ernie and Rachel have written as they have walked through the 'valley of the shadow of death' that demonstrates their deep love for one another and their faith in God."

Rachel recently remarried and became Mrs. Jeremy Wehkamp in October of 2017.

Naomi Miller (See Naomi Williams)

197

Pam (Tilton) Miller

Student: 1971-1975

Pam Tilton married Tim Miller in 1974 just before their final year of college. After graduation they moved to Minneapolis where Tim attended Central. During seminary years they added Jeff and Phil into their lives and busy schedules. From there they moved to Sauk City, Wisconsin, where Tim became the teacher at a Christian school. Pam helped with the one kindergartner while Tim taught up through sixth grade. For the next eight years they worked at the school and then, during the summers, helped Tim's father on his ranch in Canada.

In 1987 the family decided to move the ranching operation back to Maxwell, Nebraska. The XIT/Lazy YN ranch had been going for several generations, and Tim and Pam have been part of that operation since their return to Nebraska.

The Millers have enjoyed serving in the ministry of First Baptist Church of Maxwell. Pam has served as Sunday School Superintendent, directed Vacation Bible School and taught different age groups. She has designed and directed numerous Christmas programs which fit the size and type of students in the Sunday School program. She works as director of the Cubbies AWANA ministry and participates in the music program of the church.

God has given the Millers four children. Jeff and Erin Miller, and Amy and Levi Gosnell live in the Maxwell area and work on the ranch, serving alongside their parents at the Maxwell church. Phil and Lindy Miller live in Gothenburg, Nebraska, and are active in their church in that community. Jennie and Stephen Jones live in Watertown, Minnesota. Steve is a professor of International Studies at Crown College, and they serve in a church in Waconia, Minnesota.

"I still have my verse cards from Mr. Telloyan's Personal Evangelism class," writes Pam. "What a reunion we look forward to in heaven with family members, the many from Pillsbury, and other people whose lives have intersected with ours."

Randy L. Miller

Student: 1975-1979

Staff: 1976-1977

Faculty: 1978-1999

Randy was at Pillsbury for nearly half of the College's existence. While a student, he was Pillsbury's photographer in 1976-77. He worked at KRPC radio, first as a volunteer in 1975, and then as an employee from 1978-84, starting as the Program Director and eventually becoming the Manager. When KRPC went off the air, Randy became Pillsbury's Library Director from 1984-99 earning a masters degree in Library Media Education from Minnesota State University, Mankato.

Randy wore many hats while at Pillsbury. Even after the station went off the air, he was in charge of the college's audio-visual equipment, p.a. systems, and tape ministry. He wrote two college Self-Studies when they first sought North Central accreditation. He taught speech, photography, and philosophy courses and filled in for various professors as well as overseeing the college archives.

From 1999-2004, he served as the principal of Lake Region Christian School in Brainerd, Minnesota, and was the Assistant Pastor at First Baptist Church under Pastor Dave Grotzke. In 2002, he was awarded a Pillsbury Alumni Citation during Harvest Home for Excellence in Christian Education.

In 2004, he moved to Lynchburg, Virginia, where he serves on the faculty at Liberty University, serving as a Graduate Research & Instruction Librarian. He teaches research skills classes and webinars and works with doctoral students on their dissertations. He is almost finished with a Florida State University ALA-accredited Master of Library and Information Science degree he is taking online.

Through the years, Randy has been active in church work. While at Pillsbury, he served as an interim pastor 14 different times and provided pulpit supply across the state. He was the AWANA chaplain and a deacon at

Grace Baptist in Owatonna and taught adult Sunday School classes there and in Brainerd. He currently is the Discipleship Community Shepherd for the Learning the Word class at Heritage Baptist in Lynchburg.

Randy has always had an interest in history and nostalgia. He was the president of the Steele County Historical Society in Owatonna. In Brainerd, he served on the board of the Crow Wing Country Historical Society. In Lynchburg, he did an oral history project, interviewing early leaders of Thomas Road Baptist Church and Liberty University. Pillsbury closed in 2008. To keep the school's memory alive, starting in 2013, each week on Facebook he posts a Flashback Friday column with a photo and memories of Pillsbury Baptist Bible College.

Tim and Amanda (Grotzke) Miller

Student: Tim – 2003-2007

Student: Amanda – 2004-2007

Tim and Amanda Miller were married in May of 2007. He works at Close Converse Commercial Realty. They are active in the First Baptist Church of Baxter where Amanda's father Dave Grotzke is the pastor. They serve as youth leaders and Tim is a deacon at the church.

Tim Miller

Student: 1971-1975

Tim Miller married Pam Tilton in the summer of 1974. After graduation he enrolled at Central Seminary and completed his MDiv in 1979. The next summer was spent in Canada where his father Cal was ranching. Toward the end of the summer he received a call from Pillsbury graduate Sharon Wyttenbach inviting him to teach at a Christian school in Sauk City, Wisconsin. For the next eight years Tim taught there during the school year and took the family back to Canada to work on the ranch during the summers. He had the privilege of having their children, Jeff, Phil and Jennie in his classes.

In 1987 Cal decided to sell the ranch in Canada and move the entire operation back to their home base in Maxwell, Nebraska. The XIT/Lazy YN cattle ranch had been in the family for several generations. Tim and Pam moved back to Maxwell to help run the ranch and have been there ever since.

Tim's college and seminary training made him a valuable part of the ministry of First Baptist Church of Maxwell. He has served as a deacon and taught adult Sunday School classes. With the ranching operation needing his attention to winter feeding and spring calving, he became a seasonal teacher, taking responsibility for classes in the summer and fall terms. For many years he served as youth leader. When he felt it necessary to turn that over to younger leadership, he joined his wife Pam in working with the AWANA Cubbies.

Singing in choir, serving on various committees, and helping with the addition of a church building, which more than doubled the ministry capacity of the church, have also kept Tim busy. The addition was completed without the borrowing of any money by the church. "We thank the Lord for lessons we are still learning in trying to be more like Him," says Tim, "and appreciate our experiences from college which have put resources in our hearts and minds."

Wendy (Holm) Miller

Student: 1974-1978

Wendy Holm married Randy Miller in June 1978 and settled down on the campus of Pillsbury, living in Owatonna until 1999. The Millers have four adult children and ten grandchildren.

Wendy has primarily been a homemaker most of her married life. She organized the Pillsbury Harvest Home Craft Fair for many of its years. She often worked part-time to help pay for Christian school tuition for their children. She worked in the Pillsbury bookstore and library, and substitute taught at Owatonna Christian

School. She has worked at various senior living communities in Brainerd, while Randy served at the Lake Region Christian School, and in Lynchburg since 2004.

She has taught English as a Second Language courses for international students and she currently is a standardized patient for Liberty University's medical school. Active in church in each community where they have lived, she has worked in AWANA and children's ministry, in women's ministry, and leading Bible study and Celebrate Recovery groups. She enjoys being a Grandma and also spending time with her mother who lives right around the corner.

Franco and Pam (Funk) Minutillo

Student: Franco – 1977-1982

Staff – 1979-1982

Student: Pam – 1978

Franco and Pam married in 1978. He worked as the head chef at The Open Hearth in Owatonna until 1995. In that year he started working full-time in New York for a friend doing pipe insulation. He would fly back and forth from Minnesota to New York every few weeks. In 2004 they incorporated and now own Industrial Pipe Insulation, LLC. God has blessed them with a thriving business servicing many buildings in the Manhattan Area such as the World Trade Center, Madison Square Garden, Fordham University, and all Morgan Stanley properties. "I strive to let the light of

God shine in the darkness through me as I work in the city almost every day," writes Franco.

The Minutillos still own their home in Minnesota and their oldest daughter, Anna lives there. She runs the office for the Herzog/Swenson financial group in Owatonna. Franco and Pam have an apartment in Long Island where they live for work. Their son Tory graduated from Clearwater Christian College and teaches science and biology at Gaither High School in North Tampa, Florida. He met his wife Amber there in Tampa. Tony works for Mark West, a natural gas company in Colorado where he lives with his wife Katie. Rosa graduated from Faith Baptist Bible College and lives with her husband Ian Story in Washington.

Franco and Pam have seven grandchildren with one more due to arrive in 2019. "We stand in awe of how God has blessed us and give Him all the glory!"

Dale J. and Dale (Evans) Moe

Student: Dale J. – 1969-1973

Student: Dale – 1970-1974

Dale Moe married Dale Evans in 1972 and God has given them three daughters who are now married and serving the Lord in their local churches. They also have seven grandchildren.

Since Pillsbury Dale has been involved in Christian Education. He taught at Calvary Baptist School in

Lansdale, Pennsylvania, and Plumstead Christian
School near Doylestown before spending twenty-seven
years teaching Science and Bible at Faith Christian
Academy in Sellersville. In retirement he continues to
work as a substitute teacher in various Christian
schools.

While at Faith, Dale functioned in the capacity of
Assistant Principal. For thirty years of his teaching
career he coached basketball for both men and women
enjoying many championship seasons.

Lori (Cross) Moffitt

Student: 1990-1994

After graduation from Pillsbury, Lori Cross married
Marcus Moffitt, Jr. God has richly blessed them with
seven children. All of their children have been
homeschooled. "My promotions came when I got to
teach secondary level as well as elementary level at the
same time," writes Lori. Their oldest has graduated
from International Baptist College in Chandler,
Arizona, and is now a graduate assistant there working
on her master's degree. Their second child is also an

IBCS student. The rest are still learning the skills necessary to complete high school, which makes Lori way too busy to have a job outside the home.

Church has been an important part of their lives. They have been involved in many ministries over the years, including nursery director, children's choir, AWANA, pianist, Sunday School teacher and teen leaders. The Moffitt boys have ushered and worked in the sound booth.

The Moffitts live in Colorado, "out in the middle of nowhere," as Lori describes it. That has made it possible for them to have many animals on their property. While in Denver they lived near Ken and Diana Kleven, Pillsbury graduates, who adopted the children as second grandparents. Lori's mother, Connie Cross, and Marcus' parents, along with the Klevens, have all encouraged Marcus and Lori's children physically and spiritually.

Marcus Bruner Moffitt

Student: 1965-1970

Marcus finished Pillsbury in January of 1970 and moved to Minneapolis along with his wife, Marjean Odens Moffitt. After one year at Central he completed his training for pastoral ministry on the field under the tutoring of Pastor K. D. Dobson, First Baptist Church, Leadville, Colorado. For three years he served as Associate Pastor working in the areas of youth and music. In 1975 he accepted the call to Ordway Baptist Church of Ordway, Colorado. There he organized the Ordway Baptist Christian School and Singing Valley Bible Camp. The Moffitts served in Ordway for over nine years before moving to Missoula, Montana, to become the principal of Bible Baptist Christian School and a pastoral associate of Bob Allen. When the Allens moved back to Pillsbury, Marc became the Senior Pastor of the church. 1991 found the Moffitts, now including four boys and a girl, moving to Sheldon, Iowa, to assume the pastorate of Calvary Baptist Church. He retired from Sheldon in 2016 after twenty-five years at Calvary Baptist.

Marc served on the board of the New Testament Association of Baptist Churches. One of his great memories was the privilege to travel twice to Israel. He often remembers the words of Dr. B. Myron Cedarholm, "your loyalty must not primarily be to this institution, but to the Lord." Throughout his ministry he sought to live for the Lord through the pathways of life while teaching and exhorting others to do so also. Upon retirement Marc and Jeanne moved to Greenville, South Carolina, to be close to three of their sons and their families.

Marcus Moffitt, Jr.

Student: 1989-1994

Marcus married Lori Cross the summer after graduation and they moved to Colorado where he had been transferred with his job at NAPA. He has continued to work for that company since that time. In 2000 Marcus started as a TAMS (Total Automotive Management System) Representative position with the company, doing the computers for NAPA stores in an assigned area. The Lord has allowed him to receive the Quota Maker Award each year. In 2017, Marc was awarded the Monster Financing Year Award as well. Currently he is a leader in the Store Systems Representative NAPA world. He is thankful for the way NAPA has been a tool to provide support for their family.

Camping out has been a relaxing family activity for the Moffitts. Many trips have been enjoyed in the Rocky Mountains viewing God's creation. When the opportunity arose, the family moved into a Colorado countryside which looks like they live in the mountains. There they fixed up a Housing and Urban Development home with lots of help from the extended Moffitt family. "There is always more to do around the property," Marcus writes, "But that is really where I would rather be working."

God has taught the Moffitts to trust Him over the years. According to Marcus, He has done that through "faithfulness in tithing, maintaining godly relationships, walking through life-threatening illnesses with two children and paying college bills." They have been blessed through the privilege of homeschooling and raising seven children, as well as seeing some of the children take part in overseas missions trips.

Marjean (Odens) "Jeanne" Moffitt

Student: 1965-1968

Faculty: 1969-1970

Marjean Odens transferred to Minnesota State University at Mankato her senior year and graduated in December of 1970 with a major in Elementary Education and minors in English and Speech. She married Marcus Moffitt in 1969 on the same day Neil Armstrong became the first man to walk on the moon. They settled in Owatonna and Jeanne taught English and Creative Writing at Pillsbury. After Marc graduated they spent a year at Central Seminary and then moved to Leadville, Colorado. Serving under Pastor K. D. Dobson, they worked with the youth and music programs in the two-mile-high town of Leadville. In 1975 God called them to Ordway, Colorado, and then after nine years to Missoula, Montana, to minister in the Bible Baptist Christian School with Bob and Carmen Allen. From there, the Moffitts moved to Sheldon, Iowa, where Marc completed a twenty-five-year ministry. Upon retirement in 2016 they chose to live close to three of their sons in Greenville, South Carolina.

God blessed Marc and Jeanne with four sons and one daughter. All of them are serving the Lord, along with their mates and twenty-seven grandchildren. The highlight of her life has been to serve her husband, and with him serve in the places God has called them to minister. Her life-long goal has been to see God at work in their family.

210

Compiling and writing programs for special church events has been a particular interest for Jeanne. She has written Sunday School lessons, vacation Bible school materials, and stories with crafts for children, many of which have been published. Her interest in crafts and quilting has provided numerous opportunities to work with women in the churches they served.

Along with the prophet Jeremiah in Lamentations 3:23, and Thomas Chisholm in his hymn, she gives testimony to our loving God and wonderful Savior that, "great is your faithfulness!"

Scott and Diane (Harris) Moffitt

Student: Scott – 1989-1993

Student: Diane – 1988-1992

Scott Moffitt married Diane Harris in August of 1993. After working for NAPA in Owatonna while a student, Scott was employed by Gateway Computers in Sioux City, Iowa. From there the Moffitts moved to Sheldon, Iowa, where Scott's father was pastoring Calvary Baptist Church. There he was the head of IT for Sanford Care Hospital system for fifteen years.

The Moffitts are a musical family. Scott and Diane, along with their four daughters and one son, became involved in choir, special music and the sound booth at church as well as providing music in a string ensemble with flute at weddings and in nursing homes.

In 2014 the Moffitt family moved to Greenville, South Carolina. Scott began working for a glue manufacturing company, again in the area of Information Technology. Their oldest daughter Amber graduated from Bob Jones University in 2016. Erin is enrolled in the nursing program and Autumn is working on a Physics degree at BJU. Diane has home-schooled all the children and continues to do that with the two youngest.

Once again church music has become a family focus, this time at Agnew Road Baptist Church. Scott also serves as a deacon and both he and Diane teach. Since 2016 they have been graciously caring for Scott's parents who joined them and the Jeremy Moffitt family and the Andrew Moffitt family on the Moffitt compound in Greenville.

Fred Moritz

Student: 1959-1963

After graduation from Pillsbury, Fred Moritz enrolled in Central Seminary, completing his MDiv in 1967. During those years he also pastored the Golden Hill Baptist Church in Rochester, Minnesota. From there the Moritz family moved to Oregon, Illinois, where he served the First Baptist Church from 1967-1971 and then to Bartonville, Illinois, where Fred pastored from

1971-1972. In 1973 he was called to the Thompson Road Baptist Church in Indianapolis, Indiana, where he ministered until 1979. For the next three years he traveled as an itinerant evangelist.

Dr. Moritz' involvement with Baptist World Mission began in 1981 when he became an assistant to the General Director, Dr. Monroe Parker. BWM invited him to be Executive Director in 1985 and then Executive Director Emeritus in 2009. He continues to serve in that capacity at the present time. Since 2009 he has also taught as a professor at Maranatha Baptist Seminary.

Dr. Moritz earned his DMin from Bob Jones University in 1992. Indiana Baptist College awarded him a Doctor of Divinity degree in 1981 and Maranatha Baptist University conferred the Doctor of Sacred Theology degree in 2002. He is the author or several books including *"Be Ye Holy: The Call of Christian Separation," "Contending for the Faith," "Now is the Time–A History of Baptist World Mission," "A Biblical Theology of World Mission,"* and *"A Biblical Theology of Leadership."*

Daniel and Diane Morrell

Faculty: 2001-2008

Dr. Daniel James Morrell spent twenty-five years in pastoral ministry. He and Diane were both graduates of Baptist Bible College in Clarks Summit, Pennsylvania. During a year of living abroad in Israel, they met Dr. Robert Crane and were presented with the possibility of joining the faculty at Pillsbury. Dr. Morrell served as head of the Missions Department and also taught pastoral courses. Their greatest joy during those years was the privilege of pouring their lives into the students and encouraging them to live for the Lord.

After Pillsbury the Morrells taught at Northland International University. Dan died suddenly in December of 2012 at the age of 59 due to colon cancer. Diane went on to teach at Rio Grande Bible Institute. She went to be with the Lord in 2017 after battling breast cancer.

Dr. Matthew Morrell, their son and the pastor at Fourth Baptist Church in Minneapolis, has observed that their years at Pillsbury were some of the most rewarding of their entire lives in ministry.

Eugene and Peggy (Terry) Mumford

Students: 1959-1963

Gene and his wife Peggy were appointed as missionaries with Baptist World Mission in 1967 and arrived in France in 1969. They launched a church-planting ministry in eastern France in the city of Metz. Several years later that church called a French pastor to shepherd the congregation and the Mumfords moved to a second field. When that church was established it was turned over to other Baptist World Mission missionaries.

The importance of training national workers for church leadership led Gene to become involved in teaching at a Bible Institute for twenty-five years. Later in their ministry they were privileged to work with their son David and his wife Cyndie, starting a church in western France in the city of Angers. That church also established an outreach ministry in the town of La Fleche.

Baptist World Mission honored the Mumfords with the "John Monroe Parker Distinguished Service Award" for their fifty years of missionary service. When Eugene passed away he was buried in Angers, France. "France became the place of their home and hearts, and the French people, the object of their evangelistic burden," stated the citation from Baptist World Mission.

Dawn (Craig) Musson

Student: 1972-1975

Dr. Arthur Allen was Dawn's first pastor in Laurel, Montana, from the time she was four years old. Pillsbury was the college where all of the young people attended, and Dawn says, "I never thought of going anywhere else."

Through her best friend at college, Dawn met Rick Musson who was in the Navy at the time. They were married in 1975, and then Rick attended Pillsbury until 1978. They have served together at First Baptist Church in Laurel since that time. Dawn has had the opportunity to be involved in the music ministry of the church. She also teaches in the Ladies Ministry, both at the church and at Inter Mountain Baptist Fellowship state meetings. They have two children, a daughter and a son, who are serving in their churches. Four granddaughters bring them great joy.

Dawn recently retired from twenty years of working as a receptionist for Langlas and Associates, General Contractors in Billings, Montana.

Rick Musson

Student: 1976-1978

Rick Musson served three years in the United States Navy before attending Pillsbury. He married Dawn Craig, from Laurel, Montana in 1975. They returned to Laurel from Owatonna where he worked several jobs before becoming a police officer in 1983. In 1998 he was appointed Chief of Police. After twenty years in that position, Rick retired from the force in 2018.

God has given the Mussons two children, Amy, and Rick, Jr. He counts it a tremendous blessing to have served as the music minister at First Baptist Church of Laurel since 1995. "Directing the choir is truly the highlight of that position," writes Rick. Dawn serves in the music ministry as organist and pianist.

Greg and Luann Mutsch

Student: Greg – 1974-1977

Student: Luann – 1975-1979

Faculty: 1978-1987

Greg Mutsch completed his BA at Pillsbury and an MDiv from Central Seminary. He holds two earned doctorates, a Doctor of Education degree from Bob Jones University and a Doctor of Ministry degree from Trinity International University. While at Pillsbury Greg served as Assistant to the President.

From Owatonna the Mutsch family moved to Denver, Colorado, where Dr. Mutsch became the pastor of Beth Eden Baptist Church. He served several years as Vice-President for Administration at Pensacola Christian College and then became the Executive Director of Business Administration at Accelerated Christian Education. At the present time he is the Senior Pastor of Bible Baptist Church of Hendersonville, Tennessee.

Luann has served capably alongside her husband in all those ministries. In addition to her work at Bible Baptist Church she teaches music as an adjunct faculty member at Welch College.

Maxine Nelson (See Maxine Fisher)

Suzanne Newton (See David and Suzanne Rogers)

Diane Nord (See Doug and Diane Bookman)

Carolyn Norgaard (See Carolyn Van Loh)

Sally Nupson (See Larry and Sally Johnson)

Arthur and Marie (Toews) Odens

Board of Trustees: 1957-1982

Arthur Odens served several Minnesota Baptist
Association churches as pastor. He accepted the
challenge of serving on the Pillsbury Board by
becoming involved in the lives of students from the
college. They were always welcome to serve on
extension in the churches he pastored. Those who came
found a home away from home in the parsonage, hosted
by Dr. Odens and his wife Marie. Many young men
obtained valuable hands-on education by working side-
by-side with Arthur Odens. He specialized in door-to-
door evangelism and wrote a weekly newspaper column

218

called "The Pastor Says." Pillsbury awarded him the Doctor of Divinity degree the year he retired from the Board.

On one occasion their daughter Joyce stopped in with a choir from the college which was on tour. Even though the Odens didn't know the group would be stopping, Marie had a full meal on the table for them within half an hour. Upon retirement the Odens moved to Westbrook, Minnesota, and became involved in that work. Eventually they accepted an invitation from their son Jim and his wife Jill to settle with them in Stillwater, Minnesota. That was where Dr. Odens passed away in 2008. Marie continued to live with Jim and Jill until 2018 when she moved to New Hope, Minnesota, to live with daughter Carmen and her husband Bob Allen. Dr. and Mrs. Odens had seven children and their descendants now number over 135. Marie celebrated her 98th birthday in 2018.

Carmen Odens (See Carmen Allen)

Cindy Odens (See David and Cindy Allen)

Donald L. Odens

Student: 1961-1965

Board of Trustees: 1974-1995

Interim President: 1987 (January-April)

Don married Gloria Stevens in 1965 after graduation from Pillsbury, and entered Central Baptist Theological Seminary in the spring of 1966. He completed his MDiv and ThM degrees from that institution. He began to teach at Central in 1969 and served full-time on the seminary faculty until 1976, returning as an adjunct from 1986-2019. During those years of teaching he has had several essays, articles and teaching materials published. Dr. Odens was honored with the Doctor of Divinity degree from Central Baptist Seminary in 2017.

As President of the Board of Trustees of Pillsbury Baptist Bible College, Don served as the Interim President of the college during the spring of 1987, just before Dr. Alan Potter came as President. He pastored Berean Baptist Church of Brooklyn Park, Minnesota, from 1974-1996 and Liberty Baptist Church of Eden Prairie, Minnesota, from 2001-2015.

During both of his pastorates Don had the privilege of engaging in an extensive international ministry, assisting church-planting missionaries and teaching in

220

seminaries and Bible colleges in other countries as well as preaching at Bible conferences. He considers the opportunity to teach and preach God's Word the highlight of his ministry. Another great blessing has come from seeing dozens of former members of the two congregations he served enter pastoral, missionary and Christian education ministries. His churches also became the mother churches for three new church plants as he saw the results of his burden for planting churches bear fruit locally as well as overseas.

Gloria (Stevens) Odens

Student: 1961-1965

Gloria married Donald Odens in July of 1965 and they moved to Minneapolis, so he could attend Central Baptist Theological Seminary. God gave them four children, Michelle Lenz, Marcie Peck, Nathan Odens and Melissa Odens. She has served alongside her husband in two congregations, at Berean Baptist Church of Brooklyn Park, Minnesota, and Liberty Baptist Church of Eden Prairie, Minnesota.

Although very busy as a homemaker during the years at Berean, Gloria sang in the choir and participated in other parts of the music program. At Liberty Baptist she worked in AWANA Clubs, aided in the music ministry, taught Sunday School and became a vital part of the women's ministries of the church. She was also very supportive of the work of the Metro Women's Center. Gloria went to be with the Lord in 2018 after thirty-five years of dealing with polycystic kidney disease. Don has written about her struggle in two articles published by Central Seminary, *A Long Goodbye: Part One* and *A Long Goodbye: Part Two.*

Jill (Carter) Odens

Student: 1969-1970

Jill Carter married Jim Odens in 1973 and they moved to Minneapolis where Jim enrolled in Central. After graduation Jim became the pastor in Westbrook, Minnesota. Their three daughters, Kim, Kara and Kristi were born in Westbrook. Jill regarded those years as a pastor's wife intensive preparation for a subsequent ministry in urban Springfield, Massachusetts.

In addition to serving in the churches where Jim pastored, Jill spent twenty years in various administrative positions with a large professional services firm. Four years of her life involved being a stay-at-home grandmother for two grandsons. For six years she administered a Bed and Breakfast residence for various family members, including providing care for Jim's mother, Marie Odens. She also worked as the bookkeeper for the IGO Mission Agency of which Jim has been President. At the present time her responsibilities center around ministry at Oakridge Community Church in Stillwater, Minnesota.

Jim Odens

Student: 1969-1973

Jim married Jill Carter in 1973 in Fairmont, Minnesota. He completed his MDiv degree at Central and accepted the pastorate of the Immanuel Baptist Church of Westbrook, Minnesota. From there the Odens moved to Massachusetts where Jim helped in the founding of four new churches and pastored in Springfield. During those years he founded PAGE Ministries and traveled extensively helping to equip churches in evangelism and discipleship.

Returning to Minnesota, Jim became President of IGO Worldwide Mission Agency. In that position he has traveled to numerous countries to minister the Gospel and encourage missionaries on the field. He also serves as pastor of Oakridge Community Church in Stillwater, Minnesota.

Jim has authored three books, *Lighting the Way to God, Discovering God (A Chronological Bible Study)* and *Following Jesus (Discipleship Studies in Luke)*. He remains eternally grateful to God for the opportunities in international ministry, primarily in Southeast Asia and Eastern Europe. His greatest blessings have been a wife and three daughters who love the Lord. Jim and Jill have nine grandchildren.

Joyce Odens (see Joyce Goodwin)

Marjean "Jeanne" Odens (See Marjean Moffitt)

Steve and Tatum (Arns) Ogren

Student: Steve – 1991-1995

Student: Tatum – 1992-1996

Steve and Tatum Ogren are both graduates of Lake Region Christian School where his has been the principal since 2007 under Pastor and Administrator Dave Grotzke. The Ogrens have both been members of First Baptist Church of Baxter since the 1980s. They now enjoy having their three children walk the same halls where they received their education. Steve in working on his masters in Biblical Counseling degree from Faith Seminary in Lafayette, Indiana. They both enjoy teaching Sunday School and helping wherever needed in the church.

Norman Olson

Student: 1965-1969

Norman Olson graduated from Pillsbury in 1969 and moved to Anaheim, California, where he taught in a Christian high school and brought the library up to accreditation standards. While in California he earned a Master in Christian Education Degree from Talbot Theological Seminary.

In 1977 Norm became assistant editor of *Good News Broadcaster*, published by Back to the Bible Ministries in Lincoln, Nebraska. Working with radio host Warren Wiersbe, he renamed the magazine *Confident Living* and became managing editor. In Lincoln, he met Betsy Schmidt, who had been raised in Ecuador, South America, by missionary parents. They married and became active in Temple Baptist Church in Lincoln.

Norm accepted an offer to become managing editor of the *Baptist Bulletin* in 1988 and the family moved to suburban Chicago. A new column called "Exploring God's Word" featured a monthly question-and-answer article, and proved to be extremely popular. It ran for a total of 376 answered questions over a period of twenty-nine years.

At the *Baptist Bulletin*, Norm assumed several roles. He was the book editor, the theological editor for Sunday School lessons and the archivist for the General Association of Regular Baptist Church's growing collection of Baptist history resources. The Olsons have four children, Lisa and Jonathan Shafer, Seth and Kristina Olson, Julianna and Matt Smith and Jeremy Olson. Their son Seth works as a graphics designer for Regular Baptist Press.

After his retirement in 2011 as senior editor of the *Baptist Bulletin*, Norman kept writing his question and answer column. He devoted more time to his church, Emmanuel Baptist of Warrenville in Naperville, Illinois where he served as a deacon, Sunday School teacher and organist. He went to be with the Lord on May 20, 2017.

Joe Owens

Student: 1973 – 1979

Joe taught at Ruby Valley Christian School in Sheridan, Montana and then at Yellowstone Christian School in Laurel, Montana. He helped plant Faith Baptist Church in Townsend, Montana. From 1990 to 1997 he pastored Seeley Baptist Church in Seeley Lake, Montana.

Since 2002 he has been serving God in the country of Argentina. He worked with Emanuel Baptist Church in Don Tocuato, training church leadership. He has helped in the establishment of a church in Villa del Totoral. One of the opportunities presented to him has been the organization of a network of churches to support the work of missionaries being sent out from Argentina. He has worked with the churches in the area of financial transparency and the paperwork necessary for them to be legal entities before the government.

Joe's most recent assignment has been with the churches of Gran Buenos Aires, helping them develop a discipleship ministry and train those who feel God's call to plant churches.

LaVanda Oyloe (See Larry and LaVanda Brubaker)

Monroe "Monk" and Marjorie Parker

President: 1958-1965

Faculty: 1958-1965

John Monroe Parker, the first resident President of
Pillsbury, came to the position with a strong
background in evangelism, church ministry and
education. He had served on the administrative staff of
Bob Jones University as Assistant to the President. For
thirty years he traveled as an itinerant evangelist,
preaching all across the nation and in many foreign
countries. Just prior to accepting the presidency he
pastored Grace Baptist Church of Decatur, Alabama.
Under his leadership, Pillsbury quickly became "the
largest Conservative Baptist Association affiliated
college in America", according to Dr. Larry Pettegrew
in *A History of Pillsbury Baptist Bible College.*

Dr. Parker, known as "Monk" by his friends, continued
to travel in evangelism from his base in Owatonna. His
arrival back on campus from such campaigns were
eagerly anticipated as he returned to keep the chapel
platform "hot." His burden was caught by students who
went out to hold street meetings, start churches, and
become preachers, evangelists and missionaries. His
philosophy of education was simply his philosophy of
life applied to education. Everything was based on the
verbally inspired and infallible Word of God. He also
expanded the intercollegiate sports program, bringing in
Coach Clarke Poorman who had served as his assistant
pastor in Decatur. Another emphasis of his presidency
was the arts. Participation in dramatic productions at
Bob Jones had been part of his own college training.
His wife, Marjorie, taught at Pillsbury in the area of
speech. The Minnesota Baptist Convention named him
as their President, a job he held alongside the
presidency of the College.

Following his years at Pillsbury, Dr. Parker returned to itinerant evangelism and again experienced tremendous blessings of God and results from his evangelistic campaign. Because of his passion for souls and desire for world-wide missionary endeavor, he was appointed General Director of Baptist World Mission in 1969. Those who knew him best often spoke of his great humility and sense of humor. The Mission Board grew and prospered under his leadership, headquartered in Decatur, Alabama. He continued to preach in hundreds of evangelistic meetings and organized the Christian Dells Bible Camp and Conference Grounds.

Dr. Parker's first wife died in a car accident in 1946. He then married Marjorie and God gave them two children, John and Penny. She died in 1981 and he married Ruby, the widow of Ed Whitley, a long-time Bob Jones University board member. Dr. Monroe Parker wrote an auto-biography *Through Sunshine and Shadows: My First 77 Years.* He died in 1994.

Marie Pates (See Ray and Marie Pratt)

Lillian Payne

Dean of Women: 1970-1982

Lillian Payne was born in Cherry Grove, Minnesota in 1920. She married Frederick Glenn Payne in 1945. She began her career as a teacher in a one-room schoolhouse in rural Minnesota. When her husband died in 1968, she accepted an invitation to become the Dean of Women in Pillsbury, a position she held for twelve years.

To those on campus, Lillian became known as "Gramma Payne." Her beaming smile and great sense of humor endeared her to all. After leaving Pillsbury she moved across town to Owatonna Christian School where she taught elementary students, just as she had at the beginning of her teaching career. She also stayed in touch with many friends, sending out notes and cards of encouragement.

Lillian had one daughter, Susan Sanders, who she lived with in Peoria, Illinois until her death in 2015. She was a prayer warrior, friend, mentor, and beloved sister in Christ to many and one who was dearly missed.

Terry Peck (See Jim and Terry McLeish)

Dianne Pehl (See Joe Humrichous)

Anita Pepper (See Anita Andes)

Wilbur Peters

Board Member: 1970-2008

The *Northern Light* yearbook dedication from 1985 was made to Dr. C. Wilbur Peters, long-time board member and founder of Minnesota Fabrics. Pillsbury also honored him with the Doctor of Humanities degree in 1979. He had graduated from the University of Minnesota in 1947 with a degree in industrial engineering.

"Pete" and his wife Bess moved to Minneapolis in 1959 and began that fairytale success story of Minnesota Fabrics. Working together they grew the business to over one hundred stores before selling the business to Hancock Fabrics in 1985. Minnesota Fabrics stores were always closed on Sunday so that employees could attend church and be with their families. Dr. Peters served as chairman of the board of trustees at Fourth Baptist Church of Minneapolis, and Northside Baptist Church of Charlotte after the move of business headquarters to that city.

Wilbur and his wife established the P&B Foundation, using the proceeds from their business to fund missionary work around the world. They also funded a work scholarship program at Pillsbury where students who worked for the college could receive tuition support. For many years they were generous financial donors to Pillsbury Baptist Bible College.

Bessie died in 2010 and Wilbur moved to Phoenix, Arizona to live with his daughter Judy and her husband Jim. There he met Theta Mead, and they were married in 2012. They enjoyed five wonderful years together before Dr. Peters died early in 2018.

Ben and Pauline Peterson

Students: 1957-1961

Ben and Pauline Peterson met at Brainerd Community College and were married on June 22, 1957. They settled in Owatonna where they attended Pillsbury Baptist Bible College as some of the first students at the new institution. While in college he drove back to Brainerd on weekends to pastor the Ossipee Community Church for three years.

In 1962 the Petersons left the United States to serve in Northeast Brazil with the Association of Baptists for World Evangelism. During the next thirty-five years they lived in six different cities and started thirteen churches. Each church remains active and is pastored now by a Brazilian national. They also started a weekly Portuguese Christian radio program called *A Mensagem do Senhor (A Message from the Lord)*.

On the mission field the Petersons faced floods, death threats, car accidents and multiple hardships but served with vigor and determination to see people accept Christ. Upon retirement he pastored at Calvary Baptist Church in St. Peter, Minnesota and Ossipee Community Church and also served as Outreach Pastor at First Baptist Church of Baxter, Minnesota. Pillsbury Baptist Bible College awarded him the honorary Doctor of Divinity degree. Ben went to be with the Lord on May 22, 2017.

Selmer and Colleen Petersen

Student: 1968-1972

Selmer and Colleen Petersen entered the business world after graduation. They were active in their home church and Selmer used his expertise to aid their home church in various financial matters. After fifty years in the workplace and ready to retire, thoughts turned to what he and his wife Colleen could do in person for those serving on the mission field. A contact in Belize invited them to visit and bring a dozen Bibles with them when they came.

The Bible Literature and Missionary Fellowship offered to provide the Bibles but challenged them to think creatively. If they would raise the funds for shipping, BLMF would send a twenty-foot shipping container of Bibles to Belize.

Selmer used GoFundMe to raise the $6000.00 for shipping in a little over two months. Soon 70,000 Bibles and New Testaments arrived in Belize for distribution to students, faculty and staff in numerous schools as well as all the prisoners in the Belize correctional facility. The missionaries used others in church calling and outreach.

Now the Petersens continue to visit Belize on a regular basis, offering financial advice to the missionaries and filling in for them when they go on furlough. They send out regular updates via an email site called "Peterson Family Times."

Larry Pettegrew

Faculty: 1968-1980

Larry Pettegrew completed his undergraduate work at Bob Jones University and then enrolled at Central Seminary intending to prepare for youth ministry. An opening on the Bible faculty brought him to Pillsbury where he served as chairman of both the Christian Education and Bible Departments.

Dr. Pettegrew literally "wrote the book" on the *History of Pillsbury Baptist Bible College*. His book covered the first twenty years of college history as well as the

Pillsbury Academy days. It was published in 1981 by Pillsbury Press.

After Pillsbury, Pettegrew served as Dean of Students at Detroit Baptist Theological Seminary and then returned to Minnesota to become Registrar and Academic Dean at Central Seminary for fourteen years. Moving to California, he taught at The Masters Seminary as a Professor of Theology for twelve years and then became Executive Vice-President of Shepherd's Theological Seminary in Cary, North Carolina. He also serves as their Academic Dean.

Dr. Pettegrew has spoken often at the conferences of the Evangelical Theological Society as well as many other places. Randy Miller says that his book *The New Covenant Ministry of the Holy Spirit* is the best book he has ever read on the Holy Spirit.

Cindy Phillips (See Dave and Cindy Grotzke)

Kelsey and Nancy (Sorenson) Pietsch

Students: 1961-1965

Kelsey Pietsch was born in California and grew up in Japan with missionary parents. He attended the Japanese Peer School for two years and then the Christian Academy in Japan. After graduation from Pillsbury, Kelsey attended San Francisco Baptist Seminary where he received a BD in Theology. He married Nancy Sorenson who also grew up in a pastor's home.

Kelsey pastored churches in California, Wisconsin, Iowa and Kansas. He and Nancy have four children and four grandchildren. Their son Bill, who taught English in Japan for fifteen years, was taken home to heaven on Easter Sunday, 2016 after a heart attack.

Kelsey maintains a website called Kelsey Pietsch Ministries. His passion is to teach God's Word to those who are teachable and willing to change. "Our primary purpose is to glorify God by making Him known to those whom we encounter in life, and especially to those who want to have an intimate and personal relationship with Him," writes Kelsey.

His blog is available at www.kelseypeach.com.

Alan Potter

Student: 1966 - 1970

President: 1987 - 1994

Alan Potter grew up in Minneapolis and was saved through the ministry of Fourth Baptist Church. He married Patricia Hall, daughter of Harold and Martha Hall who both served on the staff at Pillsbury, on July 25, 1970. After graduating from Pillsbury, he served for four years as the Junior High Youth Pastor at Fourth Baptist Church in Minneapolis under Dr. Richard V. Clearwaters. He earned his Master of Divinity from Central Baptist Theological Seminary.

He started Calvary Baptist Church in Lancaster, Pennsylvania with eleven adults in 1974, and the church grew to 600 by 1987. Not only did he pastor this church, he also established a Christian school with 200 students, developed a Bible Institute with sixty students, and started camp ministries that served 400

237

young people each summer. His church established four other church plants in Pennsylvania, New York, and New Jersey.

Dr. Alan Potter was the first Pillsbury alumnus to become President of the College. He served in that role from 1987-1994. Just prior to his coming to Pillsbury, Calvary Seminary in Lansdale honored him with a Doctor of Divinity degree. While Pillsbury's President, he established the first scholarship endowment, introduced the College to the North Central Accrediting Association, and chaired the Pastorology Department. Al is an excellent preacher and preached regularly in chapel.

Dr. Potter sought to make a contribution to every area of college life. He studied the subjects being taught by the faculty so that he could interact with them in their areas of expertise. He promoted music, drama and sports activities as well as academics. Travel for the college brought him into contact with churches and pastors across the nation. Known for his bold proclamation of the Word, he spoke often in churches, at camps, in Christian schools and at conferences.

After Pillsbury, Dr. Potter served as the Vice President of Development, Public Relations, and Advancement for four years at The Master's College and Seminary in California. While at Master's, he continued his pastoral work by starting a church in Vista, CA.

He then pastored a church in upstate New York. Currently, he serves as the Vice President of Development and an Adjunct Professor of Pastoral Theology at the Shepherds Seminary in Cary, NC along with some other former Pillsbury faculty including Dr.

Larry Pettegrew and Dr. Doug Bookman. Dr. Potter and his wife, Patti, had two children, Andrew Potter, and Rebecca Esterman, and four grandchildren. Patti died of cancer in 2018.

Patricia (Hall) Potter

Student: 1967-1971

Patricia Hall graduated from Lake Benton High School in Lake Benton, Minnesota, and enrolled at Pillsbury where her father Harold Hall would soon become the football coach. There she met Alan Ladd Potter and they were married on July 25, 1970. Together, they planted several churches and then returned to Owatonna in 1987 when Dr. Potter became President of the college. They served in that position from 1987-1994. Patti worked with Randy Miller in the library during that time.

After Pillsbury the Potters moved to California where Al served on the administration of The Master's Seminary. From there Dr. Potter pastored a church in New York before joining the faculty of Shepherd's Seminary in Cary, North Carolina.

239

Patti's love for nature demonstrated itself through the incredible gardens she maintained, and the dogs that shared her time with shovel and trowel. An adventurer at heart, she traveled throughout Europe and the Middle East, though her soul belonged in Ireland. Her house became a museum of many collections that reflected her travels and interests. The etchings from the Prague, Israel, or Quebec City, the Ironstone from England, and the oil lamps from Masada attested to a love of learning and a deep appreciation for the past.

With her grandchildren in tow, Patti hosted scores of tea parties, led vibrant shopping trips, biked the Great Appalachian Passageway, and kayaked the Great Bear Swamp. She shared with them her wisdom and passion for plants, dogs, Irish music, Blue Grass, and Jesus. Her grandchildren became her legacy, a legacy of a life well lived in commitment to her loving husband, family, and her Redeemer.

The Potters were living in Raleigh, North Carolina where Alan served as Vice President of Advancement at Shepherds Theological Seminary when Patricia graduated to glory on May 2, 2018. Alan and Patti are the parents of two children, Andrew Potter and Rebecca Esterman. Their grandchildren are Emily and Lauren Potter and Jacob and Isabella Esterman.

Clarke Poorman

Faculty: 1959-1967

Clarke Poorman was born in Alaska and attended Bob Jones University. He served alongside Dr. Monroe Parker at Grace Baptist Church of Decatur, Alabama. When Dr. Parker assumed the presidency at Pillsbury he brought Poorman along to establish the sports programs of the college. Coach Poorman initiated the football program and taught in the Bible Department.

From Owatonna, Dr. Clarke Poorman and his wife and four children moved to Indianapolis, Indiana. There he became youth pastor at Northeast Bible Church which is now called Colonial Hills Baptist. In 1970 they returned to Minnesota where Clarke began thirty-two years as pastor of Woodcrest Baptist Church in Fridley. Next came five years with Amazing Grace Mission in Fair Evangelism, and then six years at Grace Baptist Church in Waseca, Minnesota. The Poormans moved back to Fridley and Woodcrest in 2013.

Dr. Poorman completed his BA from Bob Jones University and his MA from Pillsbury. He took seventy-eight hours of credits at Central Baptist Theological Seminary and received Doctor of Divinity degrees from both Faithway and Maranatha. He has served on a number of national boards including Baptist World Mission, the New Testament Association of

241

Baptist Churches and the Minnesota Association of
Christian Schools. Clarke has written his
autobiography, *From Kayhi to Calvary,* available from
Woodcrest Baptist Church.

Jonathan and Elaine (Jahn) Pratt

Student: Jonathan -- 1982-1985

Student: Elaine -- 1981-1984

Jonathan Pratt grew up on campus as a faculty kid from
1967-1982. He had the privilege of watching many
students come through the college as well as
participating in plays, concerts and athletic events.
Highlights in college included playing basketball and
being a member of the UMCC Championship soccer
team in 1983. He also sang in a summer traveling
quartet with Steve Henry, Will Rathbun, Scott Stoll and
Keven Zakariasen.

The Pratts married in 1986. Jon earned his MDiv and
ThM degrees at Central and the PhD at Dallas
Theological Seminary. He served as Assistant Pastor at
Chisago Lakes Baptist Church from 1988-1993. In
1996 they moved to Watertown, Wisconsin where Jon
taught New Testament at Maranatha Baptist University.
Moving back to Minnesota he became Associate Pastor
at Eden Baptist Church in 2000 and then in 2008 joined
the faculty at Central Seminary as Dean and Professor
of New Testament.

Elaine taught kindergarten and first and second grades
at Chisago Lakes Baptist School from 1984-1989. She
received her MA at the University of St. Thomas and

her MAT in Biblical Counseling from Central. During their time at Maranatha she taught English Composition. God has blessed the Pratts with four children, Sarah, Emily, Christa, and Josh.

"God truly blessed both Elaine and me with wonderful memories and experiences at Pillsbury," writes Jon. "We have certainly taken the Bible education and emphasis on local church ministry into our own ministries since graduating from Pillsbury."

JoAnne Pratt (See Paul and JoAnne Clark)

Ray and Marie (Pates) Pratt

Student: Ray – 1957-1961

Board of Trustees: 1966-1967

Faculty: 1967-1984

Dean of Students: 1968-1979

Registrar: 1979-1984

Student: Marie – 1958-1960

Ray Pratt was one of the first students to attend Pillsbury when it opened. He played basketball under Coach Clarke Poorman in what was called the Armory. That building later became Koinonia, the Dining Hall. Coach Poorman in his book *From Kayhi to Calvary* recalls that a three-point shooter had to "arch his shot extremely high or shoot it flat as from a gun! Marty Shaw and Ray Pratt learned the trick and scored many three pointers."

Ray and Marie (Pates) Pratt were married in 1961 following graduation. Ray earned his Master of Divinity and Master of Theology from Central Seminary. He pastored the First Baptist Church of Morris, Minnesota, from 1965-1967 before returning to Owatonna to serve on the faculty and administration as Dean of Students and Registrar. He also taught Bible courses and Psychology. The entire family was active at Grace Baptist Church in Owatonna.

In 1984 the Pratts moved to Evansville, Indiana where Ray became Administrator of the Mill Road Baptist School. The next year he joined the faculty of Baptist Bible College of Springfield, Missouri where he served until 2002. From 1988-2010 he worked in licensed Real Estate in Missouri.

The Pratts returned to Minnesota in 2010 to be closer to family in retirement.

Terry and Colene (Byers) Price

Student: Terry 1966-1968, 1972-1974

Student: Colene 1964-1968, 1974

Faculty: Terry 1971-1984

Faculty: Colene 1973-1984

After graduating from Pillsbury in 1968, Terry returned to Pennsylvania to become youth pastor at Calvary Baptist Church of Lansdale. He returned to Owatonna to earn a degree in education and soon began teaching and coaching football. Colene received her elementary education degree at that time and taught part-time in the Christian Education Department. Terry also commuted to Minneapolis to pursue his MDiv from Central. Later Terry would complete the requirements for a Doctor of Education from Tennessee Temple and Colene would earn her Master of Ministry degree from that institution.

The Prices taught at Pillsbury until 1984, then moved to Watertown, Wisconsin, to join the faculty at Maranatha Baptist University until 2013. Terry taught Bible and Church Ministries while Colene served in the areas of Church Ministries and Speech. During the summers the entire family would minister in Bible Camps and Vacation Bible Schools. Their sons joined them in a puppet ministry with Colene telling missionary stories and leading reader's theatre. Terry served three interim pastorates during their time in Watertown.

Coaching football remained the area where Terry felt his greatest impact on the lives of young men. Three sports mission trips overseas to play football and encourage and assist missionaries were among the greatest memories of those years.

In the fall of 2016, the Maranatha Baptist Church of Sebring, Florida called Terry as their Senior Pastor.

The General Association of Regular Baptist Churches started Maranatha Village for their missionaries and other retirees. Dwight Turbett has since joined Terry as an assistant pastor at the church. The Prices are thankful for this continuing opportunity of service to God.

Chad and Sara (Shrauner) Prigge

Students: 1987-1991

Chad and Sara were married in Minneapolis on October 19, 1991. They had both been very active during their college years. Sara acted in numerous plays, participated in Pillsbury Players, played volleyball and softball and served as chaplain of her society and as a prayer captain. Chad was Student Body President, traveled with Heralds of Song, participated in sports and represented the college for two summers on tour groups.

The Prigges lived in Minneapolis while Chad earned his MDiv from Central Seminary. He later completed an MRE from Temple Baptist Seminary in Chattanooga, Tennessee. God has given them six children: Caleb, Rachel, Seth, Megan, Samantha and Miles.

Chad became associate pastor in South Windsor, Connecticut, after graduation and served there for nearly ten years. The Prigges then moved back to his home town of Fairmont, Minnesota, where he served as pastor of Fairmont Baptist Church for six years. In 2012 he was called to pastor the Fellowship Baptist Church in Watertown, Wisconsin, where he continues to serve.

As a pastor's wife and homemaker, Sara spent her life ministering alongside her husband in Connecticut, Minnesota and Wisconsin. She loved to minister to children, teaching them the truth of God's Word through formal opportunities such as Sunday School and Vacation Bible School as well as informal interactions. Sara passed peacefully into her Savior's presence on December 4, 2018 while receiving in-patient care at Rainbow Hospice in Johnson Creek, Wisconsin.

Doug Proffit

Student: 1974-1976

Doug Proffit married Shirley Freed in 1977 and they settled in Pennsylvania where Doug attended Calvary Baptist Theological Seminary in Lansdale, graduating in 1980. He also earned his EdD from Pensacola Christian College in 1989. Dr. Proffit served as Administrator and Assistant Pastor of Calvary Baptist School in Stroudsburg from 1981-1993. In 1993 he started teaching at Falls Road Baptist in Rocky Mount, North Carolina, until 2012 and then at Wilson Christian Academy in Wilson, North Carolina, until 2017. Since that time he has been Lawn Manager at Proffit's Enterprise in Cody, Wyoming.

Dr. Proffit spent several years with the North Carolina Association of Biomedical Research. He served as the primary community member of the UNC Chapel Hills animal research oversight committee, supervising all vertebrate animal research at the university.

Doug is thankful for "the direction of Dr. E. Robert Jordan into Christian Day School ministry." He writes, "Praise the Lord for all the students I've had the privilege to influence." God has given the Proffits two sons, both of whom graduated from Northland, and eight grandchildren with two more on the way.

Shirley (Freed) Proffit

Student: 1970-1975

Shirley Freed married Doug Proffit in 1977 after his graduation from Pillsbury. Doug enrolled at Calvary Seminary in Lansdale, Pennsylvania. While he served as Administrator of Calvary Baptist School in Stroudsburg, Pennsylvania she taught kindergarten. Her primary responsibilities lay in raising their two sons, both of whom attended and graduated from Northland International University in Wisconsin. God has given them eight "super grand" kids with two more, a set of twins, on the way.

At Falls Road Baptist in Rocky Mount, North Carolina Shirley helped in the kindergarten program and served as lunch room supervisor. A great blessing was the privilege of working in a prison ministry in North Carolina.

Joseph A. Rammel

President: 1970-1987

Dr. Joseph Rammel was born and reared in Bridgeton, New Jersey, and as a child was actively involved in 4-H, FFA, and church activities. He attended Bob Jones University from 1950-52. During the Korean War he was a sergeant in the Army and served as a Chaplain's Assistant. He earned a Bachelor of Science in science education from Goshen College. At Indiana University, he earned a Master of Science in secondary administration and a Doctor of Education in administration and curriculum development. He was also awarded two honorary doctoral degrees.

Dr. Rammel taught for eleven years in Indiana as a secondary science teacher. He later served as Superintendent of Schools in Greencastle, Indiana, before moving to Owatonna.

He served for the longest tenure as Pillsbury's President, although technically, when he first came in

1970, he didn't come as President. When Dr. B. Myron Cedarholm resigned, Dr. R. V. Clearwaters, the Founder and first President of the college reassumed the role of President. Dr. Rammel's title was Executive Vice President, but from the beginning he fully functioned in the residential president's role. After a few years, Dr. Clearwaters became President Emeritus, and Dr. Rammel was named President.

While at Pillsbury, Dr. Rammel established the teacher education program. The "new" Pillsbury Hall was built during his administration. KRPC Radio was established as well as several new academic departments. Randy Miller recalls meeting with him weekly to record his Pillsbury Report which aired on Central Seminary's WCTS Radio.

In 1985, at graduation, the college recognized Dr. Rammel for fifteen years of service. His favorite song was "Jesus Led Me All the Way," and this exemplified his testimony and desire to serve the Savior at Pillsbury. During commencement, the Board of Trustees, faculty, staff and students presented him with a beautiful grandfather clock to express their appreciation for his work.

After leaving Pillsbury, Dr. Rammel became vice-president of marketing for a Baptist publishing company in Denver and served as a Christian school principal. In May of 1997, he became a member of the Pensacola Christian College Board of Directors and served as that schools Vice President for Institutional Relations until the spring of 2006.

The Rammels moved back to Colorado for medical treatment and to be among family. He peacefully went home to be with the Lord on August 3, 2006, after a year-long struggle with a brain tumor and cancer.

Jan Rector

Student: 1964-1969

After graduation Jan enrolled at Mankato State to complete a BS in Education. From 1970 -1982 she served as K-12 Librarian for Fourth Baptist Christian School. She also taught shorthand in the high school. In 1982 she moved to Greenville, South Carolina and became the Circulation Librarian at Bob Jones University. Southside Baptist of Greenville recruited her as their secretary in 1986, a position she held until 1991. From then until her retirement in 2013 she served as Administrative Assistant or Executive Assistant in a variety of companies in Greenville. Since her retirement Jan has worked part-time for the Greenville County Library System.

As a certified Media Generalist Jan had the blessing of starting the library at Fourth Baptist Christian School. She has been a member of the International Association of Administrative Professionals in Greenville and served as Chapter President for two terms. During both of those terms she was honored for her work by the International Convention. Jan also served on the South Carolina Division Board of Directors from 2005-2008.

A love for music has been an avenue of service in each church Jan has attended. Ever since her graduation in 1969 she has been a member of a church choir. She has also played the piano for youth camps, junior church and AWANA. The adult senior choir of which she is now a member sings as hospitals, nursing homes, prisons and rescue missions as well as church services.

Marsha Reed (See Marsha Andrejzchick)

Russ and Kathryn (Lindstrom) Reemtsma

Students: 1976-1980

Russ and Kathryn Reemtsma moved to Lansdale, Pennsylvania, after Pillsbury, where Russ earned his MDiv from Calvary Baptist Theological Seminary. From 1987 to 2000 he pastored the Grace Baptist Church of Marshfield, Wisconsin. Since 2000 he has been the pastor of First Baptist Church of Clarkston, Michigan.

Pastor Reemtsma loves having the opportunity to serve God in pastoral ministry. A special blessing has been the times he has participated in missionary trips, especially for the purpose of teaching pastors in the nation of Kenya.

Caswell Reeves

Student: 1974-1977

Caswell Reeves accepted Jesus Christ as personal Savior while stationed at the Ramey Air Force Base in Puerto Rico in 1968. A Baptist missionary named Billy Dodson witnessed to him and one week after he was saved he was baptized and joined the New Testament

Baptist Church of Isabela. Pastor Dodson began instructing him in Biblical doctrine and after a concentrated course of study he was ordained. The next five years included practical training in local church planting, church ministry and family instruction under Pastor Dodson, and then from Pastor Gary Gilmore at the Calvary Baptist Church of Stroudsburg, Pennsylvania.

In 1974, Caswell enrolled at Pillsbury. He served as assistant pastor at Grace Baptist Church in Owatonna, under Pastor Wesley Hanson during his college years. In 1977 he enrolled at Calvary Baptist Theological Seminary in Lansdale, Pennsylvania. Calvary Baptist Church of Lansdale licensed him to plant a church in the Endicott/Owego area of New York. Heritage Baptist Church of Endicott stands as a testimony to that endeavor.

In 2005, Reeves resumed his seminary education under the guidance of Dr. Thomas Strouse, Dean of Emmanuel Baptist Theological Seminary in Newington, Connecticut. He graduated with a Masters in Biblical Studies degree in 2006.

Caswell continues to serve as a pastor and acknowledges that "all of my educational efforts and accomplishments would not have been possible without the supportive efforts of my faithful, and godly wife of over forty years, Linda, who received the Lord Jesus Christ at the same time I did."

Cindy Refsell (See Cindy Lamgo)

Jay and Deborah (Fitzgerald) Richerson

Student: Jay – 1989-1990, 1991-1994

Student: Deborah – 1986-1990

For a year after completing his degree, Jay volunteered as a Youth Pastor at Calvary Baptist Church of Nappanee, Indiana before moving to Elmwood, Illinois in 1997. Jay took a job at Caterpillar in Peoria, Illinois, and worked there until 2016. He is now Engine Lab Manager at GE Transportation in Erie, Pennsylvania. His responsibilities include global testing of locomotive engines.

The Richersons volunteered with the youth group in Elmwood. Deborah taught at Faith Baptist Christian School in Pekin, Illinois, and Calvary Baptist Academy in Chillicothe, Illinois. From 2012 to 2016 she substituted in the public schools. They are now serving as Sunday School teachers and youth workers at Harmony Baptist Church of Waterford, Pennsylvania. They have three children, three grandchildren, and two more grandchildren on the way.

Jay writes, "I graduated with a Pastorology degree and the Lord has blessed my family mightily. Without an engineering degree, God has allowed me to learn the roll of an engineer." Richerson is the inventor/author of several U.S. Patents including an instrumented piston for an internal combustion engine, a method of mitigating axial loads on the plunger of fuel pumps, and a piston sensor data acquisition system. He wrote "A Comparison of Piston Temperature Measurement

Methods," for the *Journal of Engineering for Gas Turbines and Power* in 2013.

Scott "Scotty" Roberts

Student: 1978-1980

Scott Roberts enrolled at Valley Baptist Theological Seminary in 1980 to work on his MDiv at the invitation of Dr. Charles Aling. He received tutoring to complete his Bachelors degree, and attended seminary for two years. During that time he served as youth pastor at his church. In 1982 he was hired as the Art Director with a Graphics/Design house in Lynchburg, Virginia.

Scott has spent the last thirty-five years in advertising at ad agencies in Lynchburg, Detroit and Minneapolis. He is established as an Art and Creative Director, illustrator, designer and writer. In 2009 he was asked to be Editor-in-Chief of TAPS *ParaMagazine*, the official publication of SyFy television network's *Ghost Hunters*. Through the many connections he made at that magazine he launched his own publishing effort with *Intrepid Magazine*, a journal dedicated to strange phenomena, archaeology and the weird. This became the launching pad for a relationship with New Page Books which published three of his non-fiction writings, *The Rise and Fall of the Nephilim, The Secret History of the Nephilim,* and *The Exodus Reality.*

Roberts has traveled extensively in Egypt working with John Ward and Marie Nilsson at the archaeological site of Gebel el Silsila. He has contributed to two anthology books revolving around ancient civilizations and produces "Intrepid Radio: Intelligent Talk," and

"The Paradigm Symposiums" which is the public conference branch of Intrepid. He also designed the cover for *Arise Ye Sons and Daughters.*

God has blessed Scott and his wife Raini with six wonderful children, the three oldest grown and out of the house. The Roberts live in western Wisconsin with the three younger children. "My life has been a roller coaster of divine befuddlement and periodic joy and were it not for my effervescent nature and fervent zeal for life and adventure, I most surely would have lost my sanity years ago," writes Scott.

Diane Robertson

Student: 1971-1974

Diane worked for Howard Johnson's Motor Lodge for about a year before landing a job with Travelers Insurance Company. She worked for Travelers from 1975-1989. During those years she helped with third through fifth grade AWANA girls at Fourth Baptist Church. When her position at Travelers was cut she went to work for First Security Title until 1996 when she moved to Equity Title Services for over seventeen years. She became active in a singles group at Crystal Evangelical Free Church, worked in their AWANA program and helped out at the reception desk. She loved being the person to greet visitors on the phone who wanted to come to church.

In 2013 Diane retired and moved to San Diego to live with her sister. She attends Shadow Mountain Community Church were Dr. David Jeremiah is pastor. A small group Bible study meets in their Senior Mobile

Home Park and they are currently studying Dr. Jeremiah's book *The God You May Not Know*. One of her greatest blessings has been her twenty-one-year pin for faithful service in AWANA.

David and Beverly (Weld) Robey

Student: 1966-1970

David and his wife Beverly (Weld) Robey moved from Owatonna to Greenville, South Carolina, where he received his MA in Speech Communication from Bob Jones University. He also earned the PhD in Organizational Development/Communication from Union Graduate School in Cincinnati, Ohio.

Robey began his teaching career at Tennessee Temple University where he served on the faculty for nine years. From there he moved to Cedarville, Ohio and joined the faculty of Cedarville University where he taught for twenty-five years. Upon retirement he became a Management Training consultant, a position he held for ten years.

Dave wrote three plays, including the oft-performed *Bridge of Blood*, and starred in three faith-based movies. He loved gardening, sharing his faith, meeting people and mentoring new believers. The Robeys have three sons, Jeffrey and his wife Jackie of Louisville, Kentucky, Jared and his wife Desi of Cincinnati, Ohio, and Jason and his wife Jill of Monument, Colorado. David passed away in December of 2017.

Becky Rogers (See Dan and Becky Johnson)

David and Suzanne Rogers

Student: David – 1967-1971

Board Member – 1996 to present

Student: Suzanne – 1968-1972

David Rogers and Suzanne Newton were married in June of 1972. He graduated from Central in 1975, having served as youth pastor at Berean Baptist Church of Brooklyn Park, Minnesota, during his seminary days. They moved to Staples in 1975 to start Calvary Baptist Church and stayed there until 1981. From 1981 to 1987 David served as associate Pastor in Little Falls at the First Baptist Church. The Lord called them to Cornerstone Baptist Church in Willmar in 1987 where the Rogers have served to the present time.

God has blessed the Rogers with nine children, one of whom is in heaven. The others are all married and serving the Lord. The extended family has grown to include twenty-nine grandchildren.

Dave served on the Pillsbury Board of Trustees of for many years. He has been active in the Minnesota Baptist Association where he has served as President and the New Testament Association of Independent Baptist Churches as their Vice-President.

Suzanne spent twenty-five years as a homeschool teacher. She has taught piano for over forty years. The ladies of the MBA chose her as their President for two terms and she presently reaches out to neighbors in Willmar as an ESL teacher.

Kathy Rosenberg (See Kathy Michaels)

Paul W. and Elaine (Eggerth) Rudy

Student: Paul – 1975-1979

Student: Elaine – 1977-1981

Paul married Elaine Eggerth on June 12, 1981 at First Baptist Church of Bancroft, Iowa. He had graduated from Wilmot High School and Pillsbury. After graduation he served as the administrator of Lake County Baptist School in Waukegan, Illinois, from 1980-1989. The Rudys planted a church and pastored the Community Baptist Church of Silver Lake, Wisconsin, from 1989 to 2001. He pastored Anchor Baptist Church in Twin Lakes, Wisconsin, during the same period of time before moving to the former Genoa City Bible Church. He went to be with the Lord in 2009.

Linda Russell

Student: 1971-1975

Graduate Assistant: 1975-1976

Linda earned an MA in Sacred Music from Pensacola Christian College and an MA in Biblical Counseling from Central Baptist Theological Seminary. She served with Baptist Mid-Missions in St. Lucia and St. Vincent, West Indies, from 1976-1999. There her responsibilities included teaching music in the Bible college. Beginning in 1999 she accepted the position of Administrative Assistant at Central Seminary. Since 2008 she has worked at General Mills and continues to be an active member at Fourth Baptist Church of Plymouth, Minnesota.

Roy L. Russell

Student: 1975-1976

Roy met his wife, Lana, at the Hallmark store in Owatonna. Lana lived in Medford, Minnesota. She came to know the Lord in the spring of 1977 and the Russells were married that following October in Lansdale, Pennsylvania. They have four adult children all serving the Lord and thirteen grandchildren.

Roy is a Financial Advisor and Money Manager celebrating forty years in business. He oversees a group of believers at LIFE Financial Group, Inc. They manage over $250,000,000 in client assets. He also runs an income tax business called Beacon Tax which donates 100% of its profit back into ministry. He has taught and ministered in churches both nationally and internationally about Biblical stewardship.

At the LIFE institute they teach that generosity is a requirement for every believer. "We encourage living with an open palm, not a closed fist," says Roy. One of his greatest blessings has been working with a staff of dedicated believers serving nearly a thousand Christian clients around the world. Continued education after Pillsbury has earned the following designations: CFP, CAP, RICP, CKA, and Certified Estate and Trust Specialist. His son Tim will be taking over the business should the Lord tarry His coming.

Carol Sailors (See Carol Dobson)

Janet Sailors (See Peter and Janet Helland)

Judith Sand (See Judith Coats)

Darlene Sandusky (See Darlene Gilbert)

Paul and Janet (Melchert) Sarbaugh

Students: 1967-1969

Paul and Janet were saved out of Catholicism while at the University of Wisconsin, River Falls and completed their college degrees at Pillsbury. They moved to Minneapolis where Paul attended Central Seminary and their three children were born, Cynthia, Michelle and Steven. After graduation in 1974 Paul pastored Ladysmith Baptist Church in Wisconsin, and also started another church twenty miles away.

In 1993 the Sarbaughs accepted a call to Beaver, Utah. There souls were saved and they saw a fourth generation Mormon family come to Christ. One daughter from that family is now a missionary. 1997 brought a move to Walden, Colorado, to work with North West Baptist Missions of Toole, Utah and pastor the North Park Baptist Church. While serving in Walden, Paul passed away in 2006 after a short illness. Janet has moved to Florida to be near family. She continues to work in Sunday School and the calling ministry. She has started her own health and wellness business.

Ernie Schmidt

Student: 1963-1967

Faculty: 1971-1973, 1990-1994

Ernie Schmidt married Gen Schoepf in 1966 in Marshall, Minnesota, where her father Milton Schoepf was the pastor. They moved to Chisago Lakes where Ernie pastored the Chisago Lakes Baptist Church while completing his MDiv degree at Central. Then they returned to Owatonna where Ernie became chair of the Pastorology Department at Pillsbury and later served as pastor of Grace Baptist Church. In 1975 he served as missionary pastor at Bozeman Baptist Church in Montana, before returned to Minnesota and Parkers Lake Baptist Church.

In 1979 Ernie began teaching at Northland Baptist Bible College. The Schmidts spent three years in Alaska at Sterling Baptist Church and then moved back to Owatonna where Ernie again chaired the Pastorology Department from 1990-1994. A second stint at Northland from 1994-1998 found Dr. Schmidt serving as Dean of the Bible Department and coordinator of graduate studies. He completed his DMin at Central in 1996. Back in Minnesota the Schmidts returned to Chisago Lakes Baptist until 2002 when he became Dean at Faith Baptist Theological Seminary in Ankeny, Iowa. They would stay there until retirement in 2013.

During their years in Ankeny, Ernie founded and pastored Community Baptist Church.

Having been retired for just a few months, Dr. Schmidt agreed to serve as Interim President at Faith, commuting from Owatonna. Since fulfilling that responsibility, the Schmidts continue to live in Owatonna near their son John. Daughter Cyndie married David Mumford, and they serve as missionaries in France. Dr. Schmidt was recognized by Faith as an Honorary Alumnus. He also received an alumni citation from Pillsbury for Educational and Pastoral Leadership.

Genevieve (Schoepf) Schmidt

Student: BA 1961-1965, MA 1965-1968

Staff: 1990-1994

Genevieve Schoepf's assigned seat in chapel, alphabetically, placed her next to Ernie Schmidt. They were married in 1966 in her father's church in Marshall, Minnesota. She had graduated earlier but stayed to complete her Master of Religious Education from Pillsbury. When Ernie pastored churches, Gen served as church secretary. When he was teaching she worked as librarian, bookstore manager, and taught Christian Education classes. During the Schmidt's second time on faculty at Pillsbury she became the administrative assistant to Dr. Alan Potter. She has served in a similar position for Dr. Les Ollila at Northland, Dr. Richard Haug, Dr. John Hartog and Dr. James Maxwell, as well as her own husband, at Faith. In honor of their many faithful years of service together, Faith Baptist Bible College made them honorary alumni.

God gave the Schmidt's two children. Cyndie married David Mumford and they serve as missionaries in France. John is married to Stacy and they live near Gen and Ernie in Owatonna. The Schmidt's also have six grandchildren.

Paula Schmidtgal (See Shane and Paula Belding)

Sherry Schoeneweiss (See Dennis and Sherry Whitehead)

Genevieve Schoepf (See Genevieve Schmidt)

Virgil and Grace (Midgley) Schuck

Students: 1964-1968

Virgil Schuck enrolled at Central in 1968 and Grace Midgley moved to Minneapolis to work. They were married in May of 1969. During seminary they served at the Baptist church in Stacy, Minnesota, the Baptist church in Baldwin, Wisconsin, and at Plymouth Baptist Christian Day School.

In 1973 the Schucks started a church in Wahpeton, North Dakota. Their daughter Jewel was born in 1974. They moved in 1976 to Grace Baptist of Cherokee, Iowa. The family joined Grace's parents, Rev. and Mrs. Wellie Midgley in Pengilly, Minnesota in 1979 and Virgil preached at Community Bible Church of Palisade every Sunday for ten years. In 1991 they began assisting Pastor Oliver Sandahl at Grace Baptist of Virginia, Minnesota, a ministry which continued until 2005.

Virgil became quite ill in 2006 and had to enter a nursing home. He continued to fill the pulpit at Community Bible Church of Cohasset when the pastor had to be away and also became chaplain of the nursing home. He passed away in 2010. Jewel had complications from diabetes and died in 2013. Jewel's son Tovino lives in a group home in Grand Rapids and attends church with Grace on Sundays. Grace continues to serve the Lord as organist at Community Bible Church of Cohasset. Her testimony is that "even though I have had many trials in my life, He has always been there to direct my path."

Don Scovill

Faculty: 1965-68; 1978-1987

Don Scovill received his first trombone when he was twelve years old. He worked for a farmer doing chores and instead of the $2.00 he was owed, the man gave him a trombone. From then on he was hardly ever seen without one.

Scovill attended Prairie Bible Institute in Canada and then St. Paul Bible College in Minnesota before completing his musical training at three music conservatories. He and his wife Evelyn were married in 1955. God has given them two children, Todd and Michelle, and seven grandchildren. Don became music minister at Marquette Manor Baptist Church in Chicago, Illinois, in 1960 and then in 1965 moved to Owatonna to head up the music department at Pillsbury.

In 1968 the Scovills moved to Watertown, Wisconsin, to teach at Maranatha Baptist Bible College and minister at Calvary Baptist Church of Watertown. From 1972-1978 he joined the pastoral staff at Beth Eden Baptist Church in Denver and taught at Baptist Bible College before returning to Pillsbury to teach in 1978. For the next nine years he taught at Pillsbury and led worship at Grace Baptist Church in Owatonna.

When Evangelist Ron Comfort started Ambassador Baptist College in Shelby, North Carolina, he invited Don, who was serving Oak Forest Baptist Temple in Oak Forest, Illinois, to join the faculty. For the next twenty-two years he taught music, trained touring groups and served as Music Department chair at Ambassador. At the end of the 2011 school year he was replaced in that position by his son Todd. In a special tribute to Don Scovill, the college produced a video presentation. "You have honored the Lord with your life and your testimony," they wrote, "and we thank you for your consistent and godly investment to Ambassador Baptist College and for honoring our Savior Jesus Christ."

Sherry Segal

Faculty: 1977-1986; 2000-2008

Sherry Segal was born into a Reform Jewish family in Chicago. Her parents died when she was quite young, so extended family members adopted her. At Illinois State University she met two born-again girls who witnessed to her and she received Jesus as Messiah/Savior in 1967. After graduating with a degree in psychology she worked for the state of Illinois and then attended Bob Jones University, earning an MS in Educational Administration.

Coming to Pillsbury in 1977, Sherry taught education, psychology, sociology and Christian education classes. In 1986 she was sent out by Grace Baptist Church of Owatonna to serve with Baptist Mid-Missions. Two years were spent in Liberia, West Africa, where she had to leave because of the war. Seven years of missionary work in Zambia followed.

Returning to Owatonna in 2000, Sherry served as Registrar and taught. She left for Michigan after the college closed and became Registrar at Bay College in the Upper Peninsula. She worked with Werner Lumm and others to enable the seniors who still wanted to graduate from Pillsbury to do so. Credits were transferred back to the school and degrees were awarded at a special commencement exercise at Faith Baptist Church in St. Paul in the summer of 2009.

Sherry retired in 2014 and moved, first to Arizona, and then back to Owatonna. "My best memories are those of knowing our students went forward and served the Lord," she recalls.

Stephen R. and Constance (Wright) Seidler

Students: 1962-1966

Administration: 2003-2008

Managed Pillsbury Campus for Bank: 2008-2014

Steve Seidler married Constance Wright one week after graduation and they used their honeymoon to move to San Francisco where he attended San Francisco Conservative Baptist Seminary. From there they moved to Cincinnati where he served as Fire Marshall

269

for a suburban Fire Department. Encouraged by the Chief to enter the field of school administration, Steve took courses at Grace College and Seminary in Winona Lake, Indiana to refine his goals. The next forty years were spent as a Christian School Administrator in Cincinnati, Ohio, Brighton, Colorado, Joliet, Illinois, Alexandria, Virginia, and Plymouth, Minnesota. Working for Bob Jones University he set up and serviced long distance satellite programs across eleven southeastern states.

In 2003 the Seidlers returned to Pillsbury where Steve became the Director of Admissions. When the college closed in 2008 he was hired by the Board and the Bank to manage the empty campus. His responsibilities included selling off campus equipment, working with the Realtor, taking care of empty buildings and keeping the campus ready for sale and use.

Steve is a life-long model railroader and has used the hobby in many ways to witness Christ. His large model railroad is called "The Little David and Goliath Model Railroad" and it provides great opportunities through which to present the gospel. He is a member of several large railroad historical societies and has dressed and worked as a guest conductor aboard tourist trains and in various railroad museums. In Owatonna he volunteered at the Village of Yesteryear, dressed as a brakeman or conductor and talking to visitors in the caboose at Bixby Depot. As part of the Railroad Evangelistic Association Steve disciples prison inmates in nine states who were former railroad employees.

In 2018 Seidlers moved to Culpepper, Virginia. There he serves as Chaplain for a Christian retirement community, presenting Bible studies for the residents.

Luann Shaffer (See Greg and Luann Mutsch)

Mark R. Sheppard

Student: 1975-1978

After graduation, Mark married Nancy Brushaber and God led them to became part of Baptist Mid-Missions in Liberia. Their first term began in 1986 and they set up a radio station in Tappi for the purpose of teaching the people of Liberia in their native languages. Mark taught in the Bible school. When they left for furlough in 1989 they intended to return to the completed station and make it their life's work. Instead, civil war broke out in December.

The missionaries who were still in the country had to be evacuated. Liberians were displaced and tens of thousands left for the safety of neighboring countries. In 1991 the Sheppards and others decided to return to Africa to work in the refugee areas in the Ivory Coast. They expected to spend a few months there and then return to Liberia. However, the few months grew into twelve years. They worked in clinics, did church planting, and taught Bible school, making trips back into Liberia when possible. Three times a year, for two weeks each time, they would meet at a predetermined location and teach classes.

After one of the two-week sessions in 2002, the Sheppards went to Monrovia for a week of meetings. While there, a revolt began in the Ivory Coast which resulted in the evacuation of all Baptist Mid-Missions missionaries from that country.

Mark praises God that after fourteen years of civil war in Liberia they were able to move back into that country. Their ministry involves teaching, preaching and encouragement. Many Liberians have been trained to do the work of the gospel and God is using the missionaries to encourage them in church planting, running four Bible schools, and conferences. "I believe that, like Titus, God has brought us back to Liberia to help 'set in order the things that are lacking' (Titus 1:5)" writes Mark. "We want to help the church leaders be more Biblical in how they face issues and teach their people."

Nancy (Brushaber) Sheppard

Student: 1980

Nancy and Mark Sheppard were appointed as missionaries to Liberia by Baptist Mid-Missions and arrived on the field in 1986. Nancy worked with the wives of the Bible school students and was responsible for homeschooling their children and keeping up the home. Their family would eventually include five biological children: John-Mark, Melodie, Nathan, Heidi and Jared, and one adopted child, Jonah.

During their first furlough civil war broke out in Liberia and they spent most of the next fourteen years in neighboring Ivory Coast. Not until their 2004-2007 term were they finally able to return to Liberia, opening their home to those God brought into their lives through a ministry of hospitality.

Nancy has written two books about their experiences in Africa. The first one, *Confessions of a Transformed Heart*, records her own spiritual journey to peace in the midst of the very difficult circumstances of civil war and working with refugees. *In Harm's Way: A View from the Epicenter of Liberia's Ebola Crisis*, describes the work of the ELWA Hospital Ebola ward where she volunteered. There she served alongside Nancy Writebol and Dr. Kent Brantly who were eventually diagnosed with Ebola in spite of following all the protocols of working with that disease. Both books demonstrate the reality of ministry situations the Sheppards have faced in Africa. *In Harm's Way* is a must-read for anyone desiring to understand the impact of Ebola on the African continent.

Mark and Karrie (Wilson) Sherman

Student: Karrie – 1997-2001

Student: Mark – 1987-1992

Faculty: Mark – 1997-2003

The Shermans live in Owatonna where they operate a photography studio called "Shot In The Dark Studio." Mark served on the faculty for many years as head of the photography department, following the tenure of Ed Cunningham. He writes, "It was a thrill to go to Pillsbury as a student, and to come back and teach photography was a dream come true."

Sara Shrauner (See Chad and Sara Prigge)

Penny Simpson (See Penny Latham)

Cheryl Smith (See Cheryl Stitzinger)

David T. and Marilyn "Micki" (Sutter) Smith

Student: David – 1965-1969

Student: Micki – 1965-1967

David and Marilyn moved to Michigan where Dave attended Grand Rapids Baptist Seminary after graduation and then became youth pastor with Dr. Hugh Pyle in Panama City, Florida. From there he went into evangelism while serving as assistant pastor at Langston Baptist Church in Conway, South Carolina. For eleven years he pastored Good News Baptist Church in Cedar Rapids, Iowa, and then thirty years at Rose Park Baptist Church in Holland, Michigan.

Dr. Smith received the Sword of the Lord's Soulwinner Award after baptizing over five hundred people in his first two years in the pastorate. He was awarded an honorary doctorate from Midwestern Baptist College. He counts it a tremendous blessing to have had a part in planting four churches. The Smiths live in Athens, Georgia, where he serves as his son's assistant pastor at

Trinity Baptist Church. "I thank God for the evangelism emphasis I received at Pillsbury" writes Dave, "and for the sound Biblical teaching from many fine professors. God has blessed us with souls for His kingdom and with some good churches now firmly established."

Larry Soblotne

Student: 1975-1979

Staff: 1975-1981

Faculty: 1979-1981

Larry was part of the KRPC staff at the college. From Pillsbury he went to work with the Bible Broadcasting Network for eight years, continuing his ministry in Christian radio. He has been able to preach and present the Gospel on Christian radio with an outreach across the country. Because of his education at Pillsbury, God has led him to minister to small, troubled churches where he has been able with the Lord's help to teach the Word and see them move back to a solid footing. He has pastored six churches in that way in Virginia and North Carolina.

"Pillsbury has enabled me to stay faithful to the teaching of the Word in a world of compromise of scriptural truth," says Larry. He recently celebrated forty years in the ministry.

David and Pam (Moder) Sorenson

Student: 1965-1968

David Sorenson walked the graduation line at Pillsbury in 1969 and then enrolled at Central where he graduated *cum laude* with the MDiv in 1972. He married Pam Moder in 1970 at Fourth Baptist Church. There at the church he directed the bus ministry and served as chief engineer for WCTS Radio.

Sorenson joined the pastoral staff of his father's church, Faith Baptist Church of Pekin, Illinois, in 1972 and served as Associate Pastor for ten years. Attendance grew to over 1000 during that time. From there they moved to Brainerd, Minnesota, where David was the Senior Pastor of First Baptist Church from 1982-1987. Called as pastor of Sara Bay Baptist Church in Bradenton, Florida, he helped the church heal from a major scandal. In 1989 the Lord led them to Duluth, Minnesota to start a new church, Northstar Baptist. He remained there until 2016 when he became Pastor Emeritus.

David earned his Doctor of Ministry degree from Pensacola Theological Seminary in 2001. Dr. Sorenson travels extensively in Bible conferences and special meetings. He has authored fourteen independent Baptist books, published by Northstar Baptist Ministries. In 2005 he finished writing and publishing *Understanding the Bible*, a commentary on the entire Bible in an eleven-volume set. Three of the books he has written deal with the textual issue and superiority of the King James Version of the Bible.

God has given the Sorensons two daughters. As a family they are avid boaters and delight in taking others onto Lake Superior and the Apostle Islands National Park.

Ellyn Sorenson (See Ellyn Luther)

Nancy Sorenson (See Kelsey and Nancy Pietsch)

Carol Soutter (See Carol Baker)

Shirley Stearns (See Gene and Shirley Young)

Marilyn Steffek (See Jeff and Marilyn Alexander)

Jeremy and Sarah (Jimenez) Stephens

Student: Jeremy – 1994-1999

Student: Sarah – 1996-2000

Former Pillsbury Professor Tom Yauch invited Jeremy
to be his youth pastor in Farmington, Minnesota after
graduation. Sarah worked with Jeremy in the youth
ministry as well as other church ministries. At the same

277

time, Jeremy enrolled in Central Seminary. Sarah worked to help put him through school. Their family grew to include five children.

After graduation from seminary, Jeremy was called to Southview Baptist Church in Richfield, Minnesota, a small revitalization work in the heart of the city. Sara began to homeschool three of the children and oversaw the women's ministry. Six years later God made it clear to the congregation that it was time to close. Jeremy was called to serve as Pastor of Discipleship and Biblical Counseling at Fourth Baptist Church, a position in which he still serves. Sarah continues to serve in the home and in many aspects of discipleship and counseling as well as working in Fourth Baptist Christian School

Jeremy writes, "We are thankful to God for raising up an institution like Pillsbury for His glory and using it to serve His purposes. He continues to write our life story in the best way it could ever be written."

Gloria Stevens (See Gloria Odens)

Janet Stevens (See Janet McCune)

Cheryl (Smith) Stitzinger

Student: 1971-1975

Cheryl married Hans Stitzinger in 1978 and earned her
Master of Biblical Counseling degree from Westminster
Theological Seminary in Glenside, Pennsylvania. She
runs a business called "Hope and Grace Counseling"
which helps others through prayer and encouragement.
She has also been involved in a MOPS (Mothers of Pre-
schoolers) Program for over fifty women.

Cheryl volunteers at an international mission agency
called "World Team," something she has done for
twelve years. She has also participated in several
mission trips. "I still use the verses learned in Personal
Evangelism from Dr. Telloyan," she writes. "My
education at Pillsbury set a direction for my life as a
wife, mother, and grandmother."

Singing in various choirs as well as solo work have
been part of her life from the beginning. For thirty-five
years she has been part of the Bucks County Choral
Society. God has given the Stitzingers three children
and four grandchildren. "I wish I could say I was
skinny, without a wrinkle in perfect health and drop-
dead gorgeous," she says with a smile.

Deanna Strand (See Paul and Deanna Leslie)

Edward and Darla Stricklin

Students: 1961-1963

Ed Stricklin and Darla Hanson transferred to Mankato State in 1963 and received their degrees in Education in 1965 and 1966. At Pillsbury Darla sang in a trio with Gloria Stevens and Kathy Budke. Ed played basketball and cut hair in the guy's dorm. While at Mankato, Darla's roommate was Gail Carlson who later became Gail Fosmark. The Stricklins were married in August of 1965 in Dearborn, Michigan, where Ed's father pastored a church.

Teaching positions for both of them became open in Ivanhoe and Russell, Minnesota, near Darla's hometown of Lake Benton. Darla taught music and Ed taught Industrial Arts. They moved to Darla's grandmother's farm, two miles away from her parent's farm and began their teaching careers. Both of them taught in that area until retirement.

The Stricklin family grew to include four children, Lori, Tim, Sandy and Chuck, and eventually seven grandchildren. They continue to keep up the farm, help Darla's mother, Fran Hanson and spend winters in St. Petersburg, Florida.

Church has been an important part in their lives. They have housed missionaries and speakers, taught Sunday School, Vacation Bible School, Ladies Bible study and cleaned the church. Darla is still the church pianist and helps with special music. They are thankful for the way Pillsbury aided in their desire to stay true to the Word, share the gospel with others and encourage fellowship with believers.

Lori Sticklin (See Lori Lampron)

Jan Sullivan

Student: 1968-1972

School Nurse: 1973-1984

After graduation, Jan stayed at Pillsbury to serve as school nurse while completing another degree from Mankato State University and pursuing her medical degree from the University of Minnesota School of Medicine. Her internship in pediatrics was the University Hospital of Arkansas in Little Rock. She completed that internship in 1989 and stayed to work on her residency at the same hospital finishing in 1991.

Dr. Sullivan entered a Fellowship in Pediatric Critical Care Medicine at Case Western Reserve University School of Medicine and then moved to the University of Louisville School of Medicine where she serves as a professor in the Department of Pediatrics. Her special interests are in clinical pharmacology research and improving medical care for children through clinical research.

In 2016 the research team Dr. Sullivan heads was granted a $1.6 million-dollar National Institutes of Health grant for a seven-year, multicenter initiative called Environment Influences of Child Health Outcomes (or ECHO). Jan is the chief and medical director of the Kosair Charities Pediatric Clinical Research Unit of University of Louisville's Department of Pediatrics.

Charles "Chuck" Surrett

Student: 1961-1965

Charles Surrett played basketball at Pillsbury and established records which stood for many years. He traveled with various recruitment teams and with President Dr. Monroe Parker. He likes to tell about a time at a gas station when Dr. Parker spotted some heavy weights and began pumping them. A young bystander was impressed and asked, "Are you a football player?" Parker kept lifting and said, "No, I'm a preacher."

Surrett holds the BA degree from Pillsbury, and the MRE, MDiv and DMin degrees from Central. He has written three books, *Which Greek Text?*, *Certainty of the Words,* and *How to Know the Individual Will of God.*

Chuck married Rosanne VanPelt on July 3, 1965. The settled in Fridley, Minnesota where Chuck became the youth pastor at Woodcrest Baptist Church. In the 1970s he served on the staff of Tulsa Baptist Temple in Tulsa, Oklahoma, and then pastored the Rose Park Baptist Church in Holland, Michigan before returning to Woodcrest to serve under Dr. Clarke Poorman. While back in Minnesota, Chuck was very active in the Pillsbury Alumni Association.

In 1979, the Dyer Baptist Church of Dyer, Indiana, called him to be senior pastor. The Surretts ministered there until 1991. Since then he has been at Emmanuel Baptist Church of Kings Mountain, North Carolina, where he is now pastor emeritus. He is a professor of Bible and Pastorology Studies at Ambassador Baptist College in Lattimore, North Carolina.

Rosanne (VanPelt) Surrett

Student: 1961-1965

Rosanne VanPelt married Charles Surrett in 1965. She has assisted her husband in ministry since their marriage. The Surretts have five children, Bryan and Cari Surrett, Doug and Kelly Surrett, Dwayne and Susie Simpson, Jeremy and Sherry Herbert and Peter and Lisa Hemstead. They also have twenty grandchildren and one great grandson.

She teaches part-time at Ambassador Bible College, authoring her own materials for the "Help Meet" class offered by the school. At Emmanuel Baptist Church she teaches the ladies Sunday School class. Rosanne speaks often at ladies' retreats and banquets. She has written a book called *She Will Do Him Good*. Their books are available at their website http://surrettfamilypublications.com.

Marilyn "Micki' Sutter (See David T. and Marilyn Smith)

Marcia Swenson (See Marcia Clay)

Takashi "Tommy" Tanemori

Student: 1960-1964

Takashi "Tommy" Tanemori was one of the few who survived the 1945 bombing of Hiroshima. He lost both parents and two sisters and was reduced to becoming a street urchin. He felt it was his obligation to revenge his father's death. At age eighteen he emigrated to the United States where a nurse became his guardian and introduced him to Christianity.

After studying at Pillsbury he worked with several churches but felt unable to conquer prejudice in his congregations. In the summer of 1985 he had an epiphany which led him to reject his vow of revenge. From then his purpose in life became "defeating what he has come to know as mankind's greatest enemy: fear and hatred that cause darkness in the human heart." He became a founder of Silkworm Peace Institute, a nonprofit organization dedicated to international peace, fostering forgiveness and helping others overcome barriers. Takashi shares his life story through speaking engagements, writing, conflict resolution seminars, and workshops.

Takashi demonstrates his beliefs through art as well. He has exhibited in Hiroshima and Takasaki, Japan as well as the Bradbury Science Museum in Los Alamos, New Mexico. He also produced a commissioned eighty-piece series at the Atomic Testing Site Museum in Las Vegas, Nevada.

Hiroshima: Bridge to Forgiveness chronicles the conflicts which have shaped him, allowing him to now express love and gratitude for the two countries which have both nurtured and wounded him. "Forgiveness is the first step toward peace," writes Tanemori," as it defines our relationship with the Divine Creator and sustains all human relationships. No matter what, you can choose to forgive. We all face this challenge in our daily lives."

Gloria (Dreyer) Taylor

Student: 1965-1968

Gloria Dreyer moved to Watertown, Wisconsin after graduation and spent one year working with the Cedarholms at Maranatha before accepting a teaching position at Panama Christian School in Panama City, Florida. There she met her husband and was married in 1970. They moved to Hialeah, Florida where she worked at Dade Christian School and then to a ministry in Melbourne at Bethany Baptist.

Gloria's husband, Ron Taylor, accepted a call to serve as assistant pastor of First Baptist Church of Mims. From there he was called to pastor Victory Baptist in Sanford where the Taylors stayed for thirty years. His health forced him to retire but after a few more years, when health improved, they spent another four years at Victory. The Taylors now live in DeBary.

Many blessings have come to the Taylors through these many years of service. Gloria remains thankful for the memories of youth group at Grace Baptist Church in Owatonna, with Paul Fosmark, and his reminding us to have "chapter and verse" for our decisions. She is also thankful for the biblical foundation Dr. Cedarholm instilled in students concerning the local church.

John Telloyan

Student: 1983-1988

John taught English as a second language in Japan during the 1988-1989 school year and then returned to Owatonna to teach history at Owatonna Christian School until 1994. Returning to Japan in 1995, John has served as an ESL teacher and missionary tentmaker since that time. He and his wife and two children have been in Japan for eighteen years and John jokes that "they are seriously thinking about making a long-term commitment to ministry here." He teaches ESL at a national medical university and serves as an elder in an international church. "I ended up in teaching and ministry by God's grace," he writes. "Maybe the leaf doesn't fall far from the tree."

Mark Telloyan

Student: 1981-1986

Faculty: 1989-1994

Mark Telloyan was raised on the Pillsbury campus where his parents, Sam and Eva taught from 1967-1998. After completing his degree, he went on to graduate work at Minnesota State University, Mankato where he earned the MA, and Seattle Pacific University where he graduated with an Master in Education Degree before returning to Owatonna to teach English in 1989.

In addition to his work in the English Department, Mark edited the *Old Main Echoes* alumni paper and did much of the writing for that publication. In 1994 he married his wife Terri and moved to Indiana to enroll at Notre Dame Law School. Since graduating with his JD, Mark has practiced law as partner in the law firm of

O'Brien and Telloyan. In the spring of 2017 he joined
the faculty of Notre Dame Law School as an adjunct
instructor in bankruptcy law. Dr. Telloyan is a member
of the American Bankruptcy Institute and president of
the St. Joseph County Debtor's Bar.

In 1999, he was awarded a teaching fellowship in
Ireland and the Telloyans lived there for the 1999-2000
school year. In 2015, Mark ran for and was elected to
the St. Joseph County Council, representing the cities of
Lakeville, North Liberty, Walkerton, and New Carlisle,
Indiana.

Samuel and Eva (Hack) Telloyan

Student: Sam – 1960-1962

Student: Eva – 1959-1962

Faculty: 1967-1998

Sam grew up, as he loved to say, "in the shadow of
Wrigley field." He enrolled at Pillsbury after
completing three years at Moody Bible Institute. Eva
Hack came a year earlier having already earned her
nursing degree. Sam was active in athletics during his
student days, but his focus was always on extension and
the mission prayer bands. After graduation the
Telloyans were accepted by Baptist World Mission to
go to Iran. Then in 1967 after a service at Fourth
Baptist, Dr. Cedarholm approached Sam with an offer
to teach missions at Pillsbury for one year. Sam
continued in that position as head of the Missions
department until 1998, training and encouraging

hundreds of young people to prepare for missionary service. Eva worked in the bookstore.

Students remember Sam Telloyan for his humility, godliness, and sense of humor. Before a test he would often make a remark such as, "Well, my friends, the Chicago Bears were put to the test yesterday and they failed. Let's see how you do."

In addition to Mission courses, Sam was known for his Personal Evangelism course, and the memorization of Scripture. Students who took that class can still remember the verses which they memorized and used in preparation for evangelism.

Since leaving Pillsbury Sam has continued an itinerant preaching ministry both at home and overseas. His testimony is that "coming to Pillsbury changed and enriched my life."

Each of Sam and Eva's children graduated from Pillsbury. Mark became a lawyer and adjunct professor at Notre Dame. John teaches English at a medical university and ministers in an English-speaking church in Japan. Naomi married Tim Van Loh. Tim served as Dean of Students at Pillsbury and now pastors a church in Michigan.

Peggy Terry (See Gene and Peggy Mumford)

Carol Thomas

Student: 1972-1976

Carol Thomas graduated from Pillsbury in 1976 after doing her student teaching in Cody, Wyoming. She had always dreamed of being a teacher and in 1978 began working as an Activity Aide at the Center for the Blind in her hometown. In the 1980s she earned her New Jersey Teaching Certification and began teaching in a Christian School in Hammonton. When the school closed in 1986 she moved to Davenport, Iowa, to teach kindergarten for five years.

Moving to Omaha in 1991, Carol discovered that telemarketing was not what she was created to do, but she did interline some Braille for a school district, tutor students and volunteer in two Christian schools. A lifelong desire to teach the blind began to be realized in 1999 when she was accepted into Florida State University to complete classwork for the Teaching Visually Impaired Program.

Teaching opportunities in Florida and Pennsylvania provided Carol the opportunity to work with individuals who had suffered a significant vision loss in adulthood. Eventually she located in Daytona Beach where she worked with the Agency for the Blind and volunteered at the Library for the Blind and the Center for the Visually Impaired. While there she took up rowing and along with a companion took first place in a competitive race.

Currently Carol lives in a retirement community with the goal of "educating the public regarding blindness," as she describes it. "My parents, the faculty and staff at Pillsbury, and others throughout my life have held high expectations of me," Carol writes. "The Lord continues to hold me up and to expect my best which is exactly what I hope to give to Him."

Pam Tilton (See Pam Miller)

Patricia Ann (Whitten) Thomas

Student: 1962-1966

Patricia Whitten moved to Greenville, South Carolina to take post-graduate courses at Bob Jones and then taught second grade at Norwood Baptist Christian School in Cincinnati, Ohio from 1967-1969. Dr. Mitchell Seidler was the pastor at Norwood Baptist. In 1970 she married Ken Thomas.

From 1973-1977 the Thomas family lived in Chattanooga, Tennessee, where Ken attended Tennessee Temple Seminary. In 1978 he accepted the pastorate of McCullough Grove Baptist Church in Oakland City, Indiana where he stayed until retirement in 2014. In that year they moved to Statesville, North Carolina to be close to family.

God has blessed Patricia and Ken with three children, all of whom are serving God actively in their local churches. Through the years God has opened multiple doors of opportunity for Patricia to minister in teaching the Word to all ages. She has worked with vocal and keyboard musicians, coaching students and arranging music. She has also worked with speech and drama students and enjoyed the privilege of going on several mission trips. "My greatest joy has been to work as a team with my pastor husband," she writes.

Julia Tindall (See Julia Bloom)

Brad and Susan (Smith) Turner

Student: Brad – 1984-1987

Student: Susan – 1985-1988

Brad Turner and Susan Smith were married in 1988 and moved to Lansdale, Pennsylvania where Brad enrolled at Calvary Baptist Seminary. He graduated in 1993 with an MDiv degree. While in seminary the Turners had three children; Elizabeth, Emily and Nicholas.

In 1996 Brad and Susan and family returned to his home state of Colorado to plant the Bethel Baptist Church of Aurora. Brad has continued to pastor the church since that time. They have an active Pro-Teens program and participate in the summer ministry of Singing Valley Bible Camp, founded by Pillsbury alumnus Marc Moffitt.

Nick and Bette Uwarow

Faculty: 1970-1972

Nick Uwarow taught Spanish at Pillsbury. "We loved our ministry at Pillsbury," he writes. "We were fresh out of college and this was our first ministry." He and Bette remember particularly the great friends and mentors God gave them in Bob Eiseman, Russell Dell, Wayne Deckert, Terry Price and Harold Hall.

The Uwarows have been at Bob Jones University for thirty-four years. They taught first at Bob Jones Academy for nine years and have been on the University faculty since that time. Bette has worked for Bob Jones University Press, LINC, and the University Alumni Association. Together they have led numerous

University mission teams to minister in Ukraine. The Uwarows have been involved in the Spanish ministry at Hampton Park Baptist Church for many years. They have three children. Burton and his wife serve on the faculty at BJU. Tanya and her family own a creative design business and are active in their church. Peter pastors a church in California.

Carolyn (Norgaard) Van Loh

Student: 1964-1966

Faculty: 2004-2008

Carolyn transferred to Mankato where she completed work for her BA degree. She married David Van Loh in 1968 and they settled in Greenville, South Carolina. While there, she taught freshman English and earned the MEd from Clemson University.

From 1972 to 1982 the Van Lohs served under John Ballentine at Bryant Avenue Church and School. Then in 1982 they returned to the family farm in Westbrook, Minnesota. Their sons, Tim and Dan, graduated from Christian School and attended Pillsbury where they met their wives. Tim married Naomi Telloyan and Dan married Natasha Mason. Carolyn and Dave are active members of Immanuel Baptist Church in Westbrook.

In 2002, Carolyn became a human-interest writer for the Westbook/Walnut Grove *Sentinel Tribune*. Two years later she began editing a new bi-weekly farm paper, an experience which prepared her for her present position as editor of the local paper in Westbrook.

From 2004 to 2008, she commuted to Owatonna to teach as an adjunct professor in English. While there she wrote two books. *Great Is Thy Faithfulness*, a fifty-year history of Pillsbury was published in 2006. *Strong Roots: The 90 Year History of the Minnesota Farm Bureau*, came out in 2008. At Pillsbury she was honored with the Alumni Association Citation and a Faculty of the Year Award.

Another book, called *A Place of Interest*, records the John and Betty Van Loh family history. Serving as editor of the local paper has provided Carolyn with the opportunity to share spiritual encouragement in her editorials. The Van Lohs have made four trips to mission fields, two of them to visit Paul and Susan Van Loh in Brazil, and two to Japan to visit Tim and Naomi.

David Van Loh

Student: 1964-1965

Dave transferred to the Vo-Tech in Mankato and then to Bob Jones University after marrying Carolyn Norgaard in 1968. He served at Bryant Avenue Baptist in Minneapolis as an assistant to John Ballentine for ten years. In 1982 the Van Lohs returned to the family farm in Westbrook, Minnesota where Dave grew corn and soybeans until retirement in 2016. That same year he retired from thirty years of service as a local EMT volunteer.

Retirement simply meant a change of responsibilities. He is still active in the Minnesota Farm Bureau and the Lions organization. He holds a part-time job as property assessor out of the Nobles County as well as covering a few townships in Murray County.

Dave is an active member of Immanuel Baptist in Westbrook. He serves in the music ministry, runs camera video for the Sunday services which air on the local cable TV channel, and performs any other projects where his expertise is needed. While serving as an EMT he often had the privilege of conversing about spiritual matters with those being transferred to Sioux Falls.

The Van Lohs traveled to Brazil twice to visit Paul and Susan Van Loh's ministry there. They were also able to see Tom and Penny Latham and Bill and Dorothy Kettlewell. In 1997 they went to Japan to see their firstborn granddaughter and then in 1999 brought a United States Christmas to Tim and Naomi Vah Loh's Japanese friends.

Paul and Susan (McClain) Van Loh

Student: Paul – 1972-1977

Student: Susan – 1974-1978

Paul and Susan Van Loh joined Baptist Mid-Missions as missionaries to Brazil in1978 and have completed forty years of service in that country. Their first term they taught at a school for Missionary Kids in Fortaleza. In 1986 they moved to south Brazil to teach in the BMM Bible Institute. There they developed the music program giving special emphasis to teaching biblical principles of worship music. In 2000 they began a new music ministry called *Voz de Melodia* or

Voice of Melody. That led to the production of a hymnal in 2004 which is in its fourth printing and is used throughout the churches of Brazil. Their music ministry also produced Christmas cantatas and other CDs. One was a recording in Portuguese of Majesty Music's Patch the Pirate, *Mount Zion Marathon.*

During their time in Brazil the Van Lohs have been active in church planting ministries, turning each church over to Brazilian pastors. Pillsbury awarded Paul the "Outstanding Musicianship Award" in 1976. At that time he had no idea how God would use them in the development of church music in Brazil. "There is no greater joy than seeing lost souls come to Christ and get established in the local church," says Paul. "Our life-long ministry in missions was indeed much more rewarding than when the award was given at Pillsbury."

Rosanne VanPelt (See Rosanne Surrett)

Wayne Vawter

Student: 1966-1968

Wayne completed his training with a BA in Bible and Pastoral Studies at Maranatha. His home church, Calvary Baptist in Normal, Illinois, licensed him to the gospel ministry in 1970. That fall he enrolled at San Francisco Baptist Theological Seminary and spent two years there before transferring to Central Seminary to finish his MDiv.

In 1972 he married Carole Ann Bohren. God has blessed their marriage with five children, four boys and a girl, as well as twelve grandchildren.

During his years at Central he served as Assistant Pastor at Faith Baptist in St. Paul and was ordained there in 1975. He became senior pastor of First Baptist Church in Plainfield, Illinois, in 1976. Moving to Wisconsin in 1980 he pastored Bible Baptist Church in Portage and became Administrator of Bible Baptist Christian Academy. Wayne's ministry continued at Rock Lake Baptist Church in Lake Mills, Wisconsin, from 1987-2001.

The Wisconsin Fellowship of Baptist Churches asked Wayne to be State Director in 2001, where he continues to serve, working with over 100 churches. Maranatha Baptist University selected him as Pastoral Alumnus for the year in 1994. He has served as an Advanced EMT for 23 years and was honored as EMT of the year for Lake Mills in 1999, and for both Lake Mills Legion Post and Jefferson County in 2011.

Todd Wagner

Student: 1988-1992

Todd attended Viroqua Christian School in Sparta, Wisconsin. He graduated from Pillsbury in 1992 with degrees in Business and Bible. While there he played football. After college he worked at Amtelco as a computer technician for ten years.

In 1999, Todd was diagnosed with Parkinson's disease. He passed away in 2013.

Troy Wagner

Student: 1994-1998

Troy participated in the Pillsbury Players under the direction of John Katsion while a student at Pillsbury. He is remembered for his kind and gentle spirit, mixed with a large dose of humor. He was diagnosed with Parkinson's disease in 2007 and his wife Tonya provided loving care for him throughout the years.

Troy died from the complications of Parkinson's in 2018 leaving behind his wife and son Jude. His brother, Pastor Chad Wagner, of the Lighthouse Baptist Church in Viroqua, Wisconsin, officiated at the funeral.

Jim "JD" Walker

Student: 1979-1984

Upon leaving Pillsbury Jim, better known as JD, enrolled in a graduate program at Bob Jones. During graduate school he worked his way up into grocery store management and was well on the way into a career in the grocery business. Instead the Lord led him to apply for a position at the University where he has been serving in the Financial Service Office as Purchasing Manager for the past twenty-eight years.

Jim's and his wife have been married for thirty-three years. She reaches out to numerous homes across the country as a Homeschool Distance Learning Teacher. God has blessed the Walkers with two wonderful children who are both married and seeking the Lord's leading in their lives. He has been a member of Faith Baptist Church in Taylors, South Carolina since 1985 and has had the privilege to serve on various boards, committees and ministries within the church. The most rewarding ministry has been with *Freedom That Lasts*, an addiction ministry. There he has seen lives transformed, moving from almost certain death to life everlasting and hope eternal.

Barbara Walley

Faculty: 1970-1985

Barbara (Bandy) Walley attended Northern Illinois University to major in teaching English. She served as editor of the yearbook and President of the Student Body. She met Bruce Walley, who was a licensed pilot studying Industrial Arts. Bruce went into the Navy after graduation and Barbara earned her MA in English from the University of Illinois. They were married in

1961 and settled on a navy base in Rhode Island. While her husband was away on countless air sorties, Barbara began attending a Baptist church and became a born-again believer. Bruce had been saved earlier in life but had not been discipled.

Moving to Menomonie, Wisconsin, the Walleys accepted teaching jobs at Stout State University. Bruce began work on a doctorate and continued to serve in the naval reserve. He was the navigator for the Neptune, a large reconnaissance aircraft. On February 11, 1969, while flying through a torrential storm in the Santa Ana Mountains of southern California, they crashed into a mountain and all seven crew members died.

Barbara, left with two small children, finished her year in Wisconsin and took a teaching position at Pillsbury. While there she taught English, raised her two children, and built the library at Owatonna Christian School from the ground up. When her daughter Sue graduated from high school they moved to Greenville, South Carolina. Barbara taught high school English at Southside Christian School for four years. Then, she and Sue both accepted teaching positions at Calvary Baptist School in Lansdale, Pennsylvania, where she stayed until she retired. She also served as librarian and built up their library.

After moving to Colorado to be closer to her son Mike and his family, Barbara was diagnosed with dementia. She resided in a memory care home for several years before passing away in 2016.

Jason and Beth (Holmes) Webster

Students: 1992-1993

Jason married Beth Holmes in October of 1993. "When we were first married, honestly, God was not a big priority," writes Beth. After a few years they realized the need for being part of a church fellowship and began attending Fourth Baptist. They have now been at Fourth for over eighteen years. After a short time in the nursery and with AWANA they became involved with the youth ministry where they have served for the last seventeen years.

Beth has coached the girls' volleyball team at Fourth Baptist Christian School for twelve years and assisted in coaching the girls' basketball team for eight years. Jason has been the head coach for the boys' basketball team for eight years.

God has given the Websters four children. Jason owns four retail stores that sell strategic and collectible games. Beth works as a receptionist for a law firm. "We are so thankful for our time at Pillsbury and for both of our families encouraging us to attend there, and to serve God with our lives," they write.

Dennis and Sherry (Shoeneweiss) Whitehead

Student: Dennis –1960-1964

Student: Sherry – 1960-1964

Dennis grew up on a farm near Fairmont, Minnesota. He met his wife, Sherry Schoeneweiss, at Pillsbury and they were married in 1963. While at college, Dennis worked for the Mason Bus Company during the year, and Fairmont Canning Company in the summers. After graduation, the Whiteheads moved to Minneapolis to attend Central. Dr. Clearwaters asked him to be General Manager of WCTS Radio in 1968 and he graduated in 1969.

Dennis helped take the radio studio through many changes and moves. He loved playing with new electronic equipment and offered the knowledge God gave him to many churches in the form of improving or repairing public address systems. He retired from WCTS in 2006 and moved to Maranatha Village in Sebring, Florida. There he taught several semesters of Radio Communications at Clearwater Christian College.

A lifetime member of the NRA, Dennis taught gun safety classes at youth camps and in the communities where they lived. His interest in the rights of hunters and their safety was very important to him. Even more important, was family. Dennis and Sherry celebrated fifty years of marriage in 2013. They enjoyed many long weekends together at Camp Koronis, returning to the family farm in Fairmont for holidays and Thanksgivings in Illinois with Sherry's family.

The Whitehead's had two sons, Scott and his wife Joy of Jordan, Minnesota, and Andrew, of Waseca, Minnesota. Their daughter Lisa Buchanan and her husband Woody live in Owatonna. Dennis went to be with his precious Lord and Savior on October 25, 2013. He wrote his own obituary, closing with these words, "Goodbye for now from the Radio Guy! See you soon!"

Doug Whitley

Faculty: 1980-1987

Doug Whitley graduated from Bob Jones with a BA in speech in 1978 and an MA in dramatic production in 1980. He married Cheryl Ann Livingood that summer and they moved to Owatonna to begin his first teaching position. He was chairman of the Speech Department, directed the college plays and coached soccer. The soccer team went to nationals during those years.

After leaving Pillsbury, Doug taught speech at Southside Christian School in Greenville, South Carolina, and directed their special programs. He began his present ministry *Preachers of the Past* in August of 1990. Characters he has portrayed include Dwight L. Moody, Charles Spurgeon, E. M. Bounds, William Tyndale, and Augustine as well as Biblical characters. When he speaks in character he interacts with the audience as though that person from the past. Doug has done extensive study into the lives, time periods, and speech mannerisms of each character he portrays. Whenever possible he memorizes and speaks their actual words.

The dramatic and evangelistic ministry of *Preachers of the Past* has taken the Whitleys from coast to coast and around the world. He has appeared in three Christian films and on various television and radio programs. Eight Christian plays have been authored by Doug and he co-authored an Easter Cantata. The impact of drama has become evident in its ability to reach souls and change hearts through his presentations.

Patricia Ann Whitten (See Patricia Ann Thomas)

Allan N. Williams

Student: 1971-1973

Allan's father introduced him to his future wife, Lonnie Mead, on the steps of Old Main in the fall of 1971. His father knew Arthur Odens because they had served churches near one another, and Lonnie was Arthur Oden's niece. Allan graduated in 1973 and the Williams have been married forty-six years.

Williams attended Central Seminary, Denver Baptist Bible Seminary, and Denver Seminary. He graduated from the University of Northern Colorado with a teacher's degree in Education.

Allan served as a youth pastor, assistant pastor and senior pastor for twenty-five years in Vona, Johnstown, and LaSalle, Colorado. The Lord opened a new door of ministry in 2000. He has been a Hospice Chaplain since that time. He also led a mission trip to Santo Domingo to help build a church on that field.

Lonnie and Allan have three children, Alana, Alisa and Allan Glen as well as nine grandchildren.

Brett Williams

Student: 1998-2001

Brett Williams transferred to Pillsbury from the University of Northern Colorado. He had felt the call to ministry and decided Pillsbury would best prepare him for Central Seminary, specifically through the biblical Greek program. He married Naomi Miller in 2001 after his graduation. They spent one year on campus at Crown College where Naomi finished her college education. During that year he worked at Minnesota Citizens Concerned for Life, served at Camp Victory in Zumbro Falls, Minnesota, and led adventure tours in northern Minnesota and the Colorado Rockies.

Training at Central Seminary was completed with the MDiv degree in 2005. The Williams then moved to Littleton, Colorado, looking for work and ministry opportunities. 2007 brought them back to Minnesota to serve as Assistant Pastor of Grace Baptist Church in Austin. Brett stepped into the role of Senior Pastor in 2011. While in Austin he re-enrolled at Central, this time in the PhD program.

In Austin, Brett saw the Lord bless the church and allow a decades-old split which had resulted in two Baptist congregations in the same town be healed, reuniting in love and forgiveness. He traveled to Brazil to preach and work with missionaries and did some writing.

Central Baptist Seminary invited Brett to become Provost in 2016, working with the faculty and President Matthew Morrell, who pastors Fourth Baptist Church.

He received his PhD in 2017. Brett represents the seminary by preaching in local churches, travelling to conferences and teaching, as well as fulfilling administrative duties. He has taught courses for the seminary in Romania. In the summer of 2018, he was chosen to participate in a scholar's rafting trip down the Colorado River with *Answers in Genesis*.

Lonnie (Mead) Williams

Student: 1971-1972

Lonnie Mead married Allan Williams in August of 1972. They have served the Lord together in pastoral ministry in the state of Colorado for twenty-five years. God has given them three children, Alana, Alisa and Allan, as well as nine grandchildren.

Lonnie continued her education after Pillsbury by becoming an RN. She has served in that capacity in several summer Bible camps over the past thirty-three years. She worked as a Hospice Nurse for six years of her nursing career, helping patients and families during the final days and weeks of life. She had many opportunities to share God's love, peace and hope with those to whom she ministered. In 2002 she was nominated by her peer's in Hospice for the Florence Nightingale Award.

Naomi (Miller) Williams

Student: 1998-2000

Naomi Miller lived on the Pillsbury campus much of her life since her father Randy served as Librarian and taught. She transferred to Crown College when Pillsbury found it necessary to drop the major she was pursuing. Naomi married Brett Williams after his graduation in 2001 and they lived on the campus of Crown for the next year while she completed her BA.

When Brett enrolled at Central, Naomi found work with Cargill as a caterer. Brett graduated in 2006 and their first child, Evelyn, was born two weeks later. When the Williams settled in Austin, Naomi served as director at Southern Minnesota Women's Center, a gospel-centered crisis pregnancy center also known as Rachel's Hope. Their second child, Lillian, was born in 2008 and Lukyn joined the family in 2010.

In 2016 Brett was called to become the Provost at Central Baptist Theological Seminary of Plymouth, Minnesota. Naomi works as a substitute teacher for the local school district, raises their three children, and leads the Central Women's Fellowship.

Brian Williamson

Board of Trustees: 1981-2005

Brian grew up in Minneapolis and entered the United States Navy where he was stationed in Bremerhaven, Germany for two years. In 1957 he enrolled at Northwestern College of Chiropractic in Minneapolis, graduating in 1960. During those years he married Judy Disch, and the Lord gave them fifty-eight wonderful years together.

Brian practiced chiropractic medicine in Glen Lake, Minnesota, and then Tyler where he worked from 1963-2009. He was a member of First Baptist Church of Lake Benton where he taught Sunday School and served as a deacon. He was also a member of Kiwanis and served on the Tyler City Council. For many years Brian carried out the duties of a member of the Pillsbury Board as well as the Board of the Minnesota Baptist Association. He also became administrator of the Buffalo Ridge Christian Academy in Lake Benton.

Following a decline in health due to Alzheimer's and Parkinson's diseases, Brian entered Avera Sunrise Nursing Home where he died in 2016.

Todd Williamson

Student: 1981-1986

Todd attended Central Seminary after graduation and then spent twenty years in youth ministry in the Twin Cities. In 2006 Grace Baptist Church of Virginia, Minnesota called him as pastor and he has continued in that position to the present time. He serves on the board of the Minnesota Baptist Association.

His greatest blessing from Pillsbury was seeing God mold his life for ministry, as well as the friends he made. "God has brought me through difficulties and has given me opportunity to use those difficulties to help others who have faced some of the same," writes Todd.

Karrie Wilson (See Mark and Karrie Sherman)

David "Dave" Winters

Student: 1969-1973

Faculty: 1988-1995

David married Kathy Hunt the summer after graduation and taught for fifteen years in Christian Schools before joining the faculty at Pillsbury in 1988. He received his Master of Arts in Teaching Degree in Learning Disabilities from Rockford College in Illinois in 1981.

The Winters moved to Evanston, Illinois in 1995 so Dave could pursue a PhD at Northwestern University. After earning the PhD in Learning Disabilities they moved to the Boston area where he became the Executive Clinical Director for the Children's Dyslexia Centers, serving in that position for seven years. In 2009 he accepted the position of Academic Department Head for the Department of Special Education at Eastern Michigan University in Ypsilanti.

Throughout their journey the Winters have been active in local churches. For the past several years Dr. Winters has served as a deacon at Milan Baptist Church in Milan, Michigan, where he also teaches an Adult Bible Fellowship and sings in the choir.

Dr. Winters is a Fellow in the Academy of Orton-Gillingham Practitioners and Educators and was named a Certified Dyslexia Specialist by the International Dyslexia Association. He served as president for two IDA Branches as well as a board member of the Michigan Branch. He is the author of a periodic column called *Dr. Dave's AT Lab* in IDA's monthly publication *The Examiner.*

In 2008 Dr. Winters received the Innovator Award for Outstanding Multisensory Structured Language Education Professional from the International Multisensory Structured Language Education Council. In 2015 he received the Innovative Teaching Award from the College of Education at Eastern Michigan University. In 1987 he and Kathy were recipients of the Alumni Citation at Pillsbury for their work in Christian Education.

Kathryn "Kathy" (Hunt) Winters

Student: 1970-1973; 1990-1991

Adjunct Faculty: 1990-1991

Kathy Hunt married David Winters after graduation in 1973 and they taught at several Christian Schools including Heritage Hall Christian School in Muncie, Indiana, Faith Baptist Christian School in Sterling, Illinois, and Marquette Manor Baptist Academy in Downers Grove, Illinois. She also started and directed a home school program which was part of the Marquette Manor experience. They moved back to Owatonna in 1988 and Kathy taught at Owatonna Christian School.

The Winters family moved to Illinois while David worked on his PhD, then to eastern Massachusetts and finally back to southeastern Michigan. There Kathy transferred from teaching to business and has worked for a financial services company and two health insurance companies focusing on various areas of project management.

In Massachusetts Kathy oversaw the children's Sunday School program and at Milan Baptist Church she serves as Children's Ministry Coordinator. God has blessed the Winters with three children and wonderful spouses, Valerie and Lloyd Meek, Benjamin and Ashley Winters, and Jonathan and Betsy Winters.

Kathy has worked with her husband extensively in the area of learning disabilities. She focused on math disabilities and has an article on teaching mathematics published in *The Teaching Home*. In 1983 the Winters were honored as Sunday School Teachers of the Year by Marquette Manor Baptist church. In 1987 they received an Alumni Citation from Pillsbury for their work in Christian Education.

Constance Wright (See Stephen R. and Constance Seidler)

Tom Yauch

Student: 1965-1969

Faculty: 1990-2000

Tom went on to Central after graduation and then served as youth pastor at Bethany Baptist Church in Grand Blanc, Michigan from 1976-1990. The pastors at Bethany during that time were Douglas McLachlan and John Littleton.

Corlene Yauch, Tom's wife, died unexpectedly at only 37 years of age in 1983. He married Suzanne Burk and they had four daughters, Ashley, Ellyse, Tara and Alex. Returning to Pillsbury in 1990, Tom filled several positions. He became Dean of Students and taught Church Ministry, sharing his expertise from years of pastoral and youth work. A class which many students remembered was the one he taught on the Christian Home.

In 2000 Tom accepted the call to serve as pastor of the Bible Baptist Church in Farmington, Minnesota. Three years later he was diagnosed with stage four non-Hodgkins lymphoma. Under treatment for that, his condition changed and the diagnosis became multiple myeloma. Tom went to be with the Lord in 2014.

Gene and Shirley (Stearns) Young

Student: 1966-1971

Director of Admissions: 2001-2003

Gene Young married Shirley Stearns in August of 1971. They moved to Minneapolis where he entered Central Seminary. In 1976 they left to help start Trinity Baptist Church. For the next twenty-five years Gene worked in various areas of sales. He sold everything from cars to appliances, electronics and clothes. In the middle of that time he taught school for a year to help a friend.

In 2000 Shirley died of cancer. God had given the Youngs three children. Tiffany married Bjorn Engstrom and lives in Stockholm, Sweden with Bjorn and three sons. Gene had the privilege of leading Bjorn to the Lord in salvation. Micah and his wife Carol have two sons and live in Keller, Texas. Micah works in real estate and Carol in the medical device business. Tierney works as an airplane engineer in Seattle. During eleven years in the motorcycle parts industry, Gene was honored for being in the top five in sales for five of those years.

In 2001 Gene returned to Pillsbury to serve as the Director of Admissions. In that position he was able to maintain contact with Pillsbury graduates across the country. At the present time he works as a Field Representative for Rio Grande Bible Ministries in Edinburg, Texas and continues to travel, stopping in to fellowship with old friends as he goes.

Tom and Jane (Elliot) Zempel

Student: 1962-1968

Faculty: 1978-1984

Tom attended Central after graduation and then completed his doctoral work in Biblical Counseling at Westminster Theological Seminary in Philadelphia, Pennsylvania. He married Jane Elliot in 1968 and they had three children, Jonathan and Renee Zempel, Benjamin Zempel, and Amy and Neil Hazard.

Tom was an effective teacher and mentor and an innovative and adventurous thinker. Above all, he was a delightfully happy and committed follower of his Savior and Friend, Jesus Christ.

He began his ministry as a youth pastor in Rockford and then Danville, Illinois. At Pillsbury he served as professor of Bible and Counseling, Christian Education and Dean of Students. Tom spent ten years as senior pastor in Windsor Locks, Connecticut, and seventeen years as professor of Biblical Counseling and Vice President of Central Seminary in Minneapolis. The final five years of Tom's life were invested as Counseling Pastor of Colonial Baptist Church and professor of Biblical Counseling at Shepherds Theological Seminary in Cary, North Carolina. He also served as an elder at the church and taught the Crossroads ABF class.

Dr. Zempel set out on his routine Sunday morning run on April 24, 2016 and "ran straight into the arms of Jesus." He health was strong until the moment his Father called him home.

Jeffrey and Anne (Engelberth) Zimmerman

Student: 1974-1976

Jeff married Anne Engelberth in July of 1977 and God has blessed them with two girls. Melodee and John Whitman are missionaries in Italy. Harmony and Stephen Danielsen live for Christ in Columbus, Ohio. Jeff served as an associate pastor and then pastored four different congregations. He was at Briley Chapel in Indiana from 1984-1989. In Olney, Illinois he served at

Calvary Baptist Church from 1989-1994. From there the Zimmermans moved to Dillsburg, Pennsylvania, where he pastored Cedar Hill Baptist from 1994-2004. Since 2004 he has been the pastor of Grace Baptist Church in LaBelle, Florida.

The greatest joy of Jeff's ministry has been seeing many individuals come to Christ. As a result of his ministry, two men have been called to preach and another couple entered a camp ministry. Jeff says, "Pillsbury and Central gave me great friends and a great foundation for serving our Lord."

Rachel Zoschke (See Ernie and Rachel Miller)

Pillsbury Baptist Bible College continues to live on in the work God is doing through those who were touched by its ministry. If you were a student at the college, a staff member, or served on the faculty, administration of board we would love to hear your story and include it in future editions of *Arise Ye Sons and Daughters*. **All profit from the sale of these books will be given to the library of Central Baptist Theological Seminary, Plymouth, Minnesota.**

Please fill out the questionnaire and send it to Randy Miller at RandyLMiller@gmail.com or Robert Allen at robertallen@biblestoryfamily.com. Questionnaires can also be mailed to Randy at 109 Willow Bend Drive, Lynchburg, VA 24502 or Robert at PO Box 28342, Minneapolis, MN 55428.

Updates and corrections can also be sent to one of those addresses.

ARISE YE SONS AND DAUGHTERS

Name _____

Years at Pillsbury _____

(Indicate - for example: **Student** 1966-1970 **Faculty** 1990-2000 **Board** 1970-1988 **Administration** 1956-1966)

Email address (For contact purposes only. Will not be published. We will notify you when future editions of the book become available.)

_____

Brief **summary** of life since leaving Pillsbury.

Highlights (Blessings, Opportunities, Publications, Presentations, Victories, Honors etc., detailing how God has worked in your life as one of Pillsbury's "Sons and Daughters," during college and since.)

This is not intended to be a directory. Personal addresses and emails will not be included in the publication. Our intention is to make available as an ebook, or through "publish on demand," a volume which celebrates the mighty hand of God in the lives of those who were touched by the ministry of Pillsbury Baptist Bible College. Please join us on the journey as we "stand in awe of the work which Thou hast wrought" (Parker/Cedarholm).

318

ADDITIONAL PILLSBURY RESOURCES

The History of Pillsbury Baptist by College by Larry Dean Pettegrew.

This history was published in 1981 and printed by the Pillsbury Press, Owatonna, MN. The book, which is now out of print, covers extensively the founding of Minnesota Academy which later became Pillsbury Academy. It records the legal battle for control of the property and the founding and leadership of the Bible College through the time of its publication in 1981.

Great is Thy Faithfulness by Carolyn Van Loh

This book was published in 2006 and printed by Nystrom Press. Carolyn covers the Academy Days briefly, and then focuses on each of the decades of the existence of the Bible College. The inclusion of multiple pictures and personal testimonies makes this a valuable resource for anyone wanting to research the growth and development of Pillsbury Baptist Bible College.

Made in the USA
Lexington, KY
28 January 2019